Living YES in a NO World

LIVING YES IN A NO WORLD
Published by Live YES! Publishing
©2011by Randy Gregg

ISBN: 978-0-9801964-6-7

Library of Congress Control Number TX0007571998

Cover Image by Chris Gilbert, The Studio Gearbox

Printed in the United States of America

For Information:
LiVE YES! Publishing
P. O. Box 1319
Madison, GA 30650

LiVEYES!™

Living YES in a NO World

Live yes!
Randy Gregg

Randy Gregg

To those who live YES by walking into the darkness, doubt, and pain, whether created by the events of life, or their own inconsistencies, while maintaining hope, faith and love, with gratitude for your courage, perseverance, and spirit, for Living YES in a NO World.

Contents

Healing Souls

Rebirth

Acknowledgements

The concept for this book evolved over a long period of time. Because it has, I am indebted to a number of people for their influence and contributions. I cannot list all of them, but each one holds a special place in my heart. To each person, whether family or friend, I say "thank you" for kind words, thoughtful gestures, encouragement and support. May the journey continue as we share YES with everyone we meet.

My family has served as my biggest group of cheerleaders. My wife, Dianne, has helped me brainstorm, refine and recreate again. This doesn't apply just to the book, but also to me as a person. I have reinvented myself so many times; always with her support. She lives YES on every level. Our daughters and their husbands, Lindsay and Todd Peaster and Laura and Michael Hardester, have provided constant encouragement as well as thoughtful suggestions. Harrison, Lily, and Grant have given me exactly what I always need—unconditional love. These are the original members of my YES team.

Todd Peaster has served as a refiner of big ideas and collaborator of plans. He helps an older-generation person find ways to navigate the complex world of technology.

Carole Mathias has served as an encourager and colleague. I am grateful I met her and for her belief in the idea of this book and support to help make it become a reality.

Karen Jones Richardson has used art in therapy for years as a marriage and family therapist. I want to give her credit for creating the Stages of a YES Heart sketches though I was not able to include them in the book.

Lorayne Bryan turned the manuscript and stories into a much smoother document. She shared her expertise in a professional manner—quick, efficient and honest.

Christopher Gilbert with The Studio Gearbox developed the book cover. From a distance, he asked, listened and suggested. His creativity and ability to understand the spirit of the book was beautifully captured in his work.

My original plan for writing changed over time. At first, I thought it would be just a cut- and-paste process. I would share an idea, people would respond, and a book would be born in 90 days. Like so many of my misguided plans, something happened I didn't expect. As individuals began to share their sacred stories, I was humbled and transformed at the same time. I stand in awe of those who have walked through and stood in the dark spots of experience, yet found a way to walk through to the other side. To those who have pulled back the curtains to the windows of their soul and allowed us to peek into the places where they have been broken, I consider it one of the greatest gifts you can share with another human being. For this reason, I consider it to be a walk into the "holy of holies."

With gratitude I thank the following individuals for sharing their words, experiences and journey so that others might find encouragement:

Sara Bosch
Kim Allegood Brown
Myra Cameron

Stacye Whitt Clark
Jan Coker
April Hair Cross
Hope DeLaigle Collier
Jeff Davis
Michelle Clark Davison
Kacey Lowe Dixon
Cindy Edwards
Linda Edwards
Jill Elliott
Dianne Junkins Gregg
Willa Dean Gregg
Amanda Fogarty Hall
Laura Gregg Hardester
Foss Hodges
Charlene Wright Jackson
Stephen Jones
Tiffany Lowe Jones
Carlene Jones Kelley
Abby Miller Martin
Carol Mathias
Angee Knight McKee
Melissa Jones Mitchell
T. Mickey Moss
Carole Wren Nelson
Brenda Pike Oglesby
Brian Payton

Judi Payton
Helen Peaster
Lindsay Gregg Peaster
Jennifer Lynn Petroski
Mary Ann Prior
Karen Annette Jones Richardson
Ann Lay Ross
Betty Ryfun
Monica Ducker Semrad
Betsy Short
Brenda Smith
Brenna Brousseau Smith
Nancy Conley Smith
Jean Stafford
Lisa Palmer Talley

A First Word

I recognize that I follow a different path. I march to the beat of a different drum. It isn't one I always understand or can easily explain to others. I have come to believe it is mine, and that is all I need to know. For these reasons, this book is not like anything else I have found.

It seems to me that we are all whispering God stories to one another. In the telling and re-telling, we are trying to put our moments into words that we hope, pray, dream and desire will help us make sense out of our lives. So, we tell stories of what has happened or changed for us. In the re-telling, we look for connections and intimacy. We crane our necks, tilt our heads, and cup our ears hoping we will hear just the whisper of His voice in the ordinariness of everyday life. We want something more than a platitude. We want presence. Yet, it isn't in any of the details where we find connection. It is in the brokenness. It is when everything falls apart, doesn't fit and won't work. Then we see how much we share in common with those around us.

In our brokenness, I believe we lose our connection to the Divine YES of life. Our thoughts become, "God wasn't supposed to let this happen." Trust seems more fragile than ever. Financial institutions have faltered. Politicians offer promises but can't seem to resolve the problems we face as a country. We have come to believe ministers have all of the answers, but they don't. As one highly visible minister after another has stumbled and fallen, we wonder where our heroes of the faith are now. We go to church expecting to find a solution, hear a truth or discover help. Instead, we see nicely dressed people, behaving well, and giving the appearance that they have everything wonderfully wrapped up with a neat little bow. We want intimacy but settle for artificial relationships. We stumble out of the door of private homes into the public, but dusty, roads of life without a GPS or roadmap. We don't know where to go. We don't know who to ask for help.

I want to offer another thought for your consideration. I don't see the solution in an institution, person or pat answer. To me, it is in a relationship and a journey—sharing it with others, walking straight ahead into the moments of celebration and sadness, listening to happy and hurting hearts, finding healing and wholeness, and hearing a gentle whisper of Grace as we share our brokenness and discover in others the intimacy and acceptance we so desperately want to find.

I think we need to look at our lives, institutions and relationships differently. I believe we need to discover, live, nurture and embrace YES. But this YES is different than the one that might first come to mind. This isn't about a motivational speech or brief response to a question. It is more clearly defined and related to our purpose in being here. It comes from deep within our souls.

This book isn't for everyone. If you expect instant answers, loud pronouncements of truth, or religious platitudes, you will not find it here. This simply isn't the place for you.

If you seek awareness, listening, and gentle movements of the spirit, may the words that are shared on these pages speak the message that you need to hear.

This topic is too large and the needs are too great for me alone. I have invited other pilgrims of the spirit to share their God stories as well. I want you to hear their stories. They have walked through the "shadow of the valley" (Psalm 23:4) in many ways. They are friends, family, and acquaintances. They are everyday people.

This isn't a hall of fame for the saints; it is a clinic for wounded sinners who desire healing and wholeness. If you are tired of hurting and aimlessly drifting through your life without purpose or meaning, then I invite you to become intentional in being the wonderful, beautiful and vibrant individual you were created to be. This book is for you. Come on in. Sit down. Relax. Read awhile and then put it down. Let the thoughts and stories wash over you. Allow the waves of the Spirit to carry you to a new place. It is what I call, "being at home with your life."

Enjoy.

A Second Word

Books are easy enough to follow. Read and turn the page until you finish it.

For this one, I want to offer another option.

I suggest that you consider your life as a prayer. It is one that is being constantly uttered in the everyday and ordinary moments. I have tried to incorporate this thought into the flow of the book.

With each section: Beginnings; Sources; Entrances and Exits; Wounded Spirits; Healing Souls and Rebirth, there is a structure that will be helpful for you to know. This is a thought that evolved over time and began to take shape as the book was being written. I now see these as the stages our hearts move through along our journey toward wholeness.

Prayers: I have offered a prayer for you to read. If our life is a prayer, then all that we do can be considered a prayer as well.

Reading Material: My thoughts follow in each unit.

Sacred Stories: These were provided by friends, family and acquaintances. I call them sacred because I believe that they come from the holy of holies of experience.

Reflections: A brief summary of the section to help you capture the idea as you move forward.

In a Tilted World

In the immortal words of Robert Frost in his 1920 poem, *The Road Not Taken,* "I took the one less traveled by, and that has made all the difference."[i] I invite you to join me on a journey. It is a little non-traditional and yet traditional at the same time. It is an adventure waiting to open up before us with new directions and dreams to be discovered.

It takes courage to live the life you have been given. Rather than choose a distant land as the focus of our pilgrimage, I want to visit something more sacred and holy than any destination or location—it is the gift of your life with all of the twists and turns in it. I want to walk with you through the museum of your memory and look at images stored away that still come alive and create joy as well as havoc for you.

Before we start, I want to raise some critical questions to consider. Are you living the life you were meant to live? Do you have a dream and are you pursuing it? Where have you been knocked around by the unexpected, unwanted, and unplanned? Have you healed from the pain? Have you discovered your second journey yet? If your life is broken, where do you go to heal and who helps you put the pieces back together again? Is your life complete? Is there a sense of cohesion? Does your life make sense?

These are questions I have faced. I don't have all of the answers, for I am a pilgrim as well. I seek and search. I ask questions, challenge solutions and listen for deeper truths. I avoid superficial answers. I dislike religious platitudes. Much of the material you will read on the pages that follow comes from

1

the deep places of my own walk—pain experienced, lessons learned, and truths discovered. I am not here to tell you that you must live this way as much as to suggest that you listen. Listen to my words, listen to the stories shared by others, and most importantly, listen to your own life.

You are not alone. This sacred journey is too important and valued to walk alone. I have invited many, many friends to share the truths they have learned from their deep places. I think you will be surprised and moved by what you hear. As we examine their stories, your truth will become much clearer. I also believe the question that life is asking of you will emerge. You will hear, not the first or second, but third question you must answer to move forward into a life of wholeness and completion.

Let me begin with a few thoughts that give direction to all that follows.

A Different View

I don't remember the first time I hung upside down. Must have been when I was around 7 or 8 years old. I am sure it was from a pine tree—they have the straightest limbs for climbing, you know. I shimmed up the tree to prove my climbing ability, scooted out on a limb, locked my legs around the rough bark, and then let my body drop toward the ground. This was big deal—for a young boy. It was a test of super strength and special agility to showcase to family and friends. I had proven I could hang upside down and look at trees, fences, people, and grass from another point of view. When you live in the country, you find your own entertainment.

I didn't realize it was a skill I would ever need beyond the age of 10, but I have used it over and over again on many occasions. No, I don't literally climb trees anymore, though there are times when I wish that I could. There are days when I would like to be able to find a strong limb, climb high up in a tree and sit for hours, hidden from all the noise and uncertainty.

But, to experience a well-lived life, you can't climb a tree, hide behind the leaves, or run away from reality. You face it head on. This requires a special skill—the ability to look at the world differently—see reality but through the eyes of trust and faith.

Astronomers tell us that the earth is tilted to its orbital plane at an angle of 23.5 degrees. This creates varying degrees of exposure to the sun for the Northern and Southern Hemispheres that provide the changing seasons of weather, ecology and daylight.[ii] The life lesson I hear is that to enjoy all the seasons of life, you must be tilted at some angle to experience the growth of spring, heat of summer, transition of fall and stillness of winter. With age, I now wonder if each season offers a unique lesson to be learned. Sometimes all are merged into a single event—growth, heat, transition and stillness.

YES Moments

I have known YES moments. There have been those occasions when energy, passion, potential, and purpose came together to create a sweet spot of celebration. Things fit. There was a flow and direction. There was internal and external alignment of my worlds into one cohesive experience.

3

I think we are created for these. I believe we have been divinely designed to embrace goodness, grace, hope, love and achievement. I think part of our "sacred contract," as Karen Jones Richardson describes it, is to set and reach our dreams.

We can't live in the YES moments. We want YES; we get NO. As my friend Carol Mathias describes it:

> "Those moments when someone is banging on the door in the middle of the night, and you know it's paranormal or seriously disruptive. Or driving directly into the sun in an area that is unfamiliar, the sway of several little things that go wrong...running late and hitting every red-light. Or you can't find your keys and waste 30 minutes searching. All are the small stressors that make a day feel like a bad Monday, but their cumulative effect leaves you out of balance, bored and feeling inadequate. These moments aren't deal breakers, but the chronic erosion of self-esteem and mastery that sets us adrift—away from those touchstones of YES moments."

A Broken Life

Our lives are broken; perhaps not shattered, but cracked to the point you don't feel that you serve a useful purpose. Something or someone comes along and whacks us right off our highway to happiness. Our lives get tilted—physically, emotionally, spiritually, psychologically and relationally. I look for the road sign that points toward success, but I sit in the ditch waiting on a tow truck to pull me out and repair my bent fenders.

Everyone is broken. All of us have nicks, dents and scratches in our plans and dreams. In reality, the problem runs much deeper. We see brokenness as a weakness to be denied, protected or avoided all together. Instead, it is simply brokenness. It is the place where we aren't strong, we don't have answers and we need others to make us whole.

Through the stories that some fellow pilgrims have shared, you will read where life has caved in for many, many people. You will hear their pain and frustration, but you will hear something more. It is the smallest word being spoken in the midst of the chaos and uncertainty—feebly and quietly. It is hope. You will hear, feel and discover how others have walked their path. You will learn what has helped them, not only to survive, but led them to find a new purpose in the midst of their pain.

Searching for Magic Words

My wife, Dianne, loves magic words. As she states, "Sometimes I feel that magic words do help in a tilted world—sometimes a note from someone, a kind word, a compliment when I was unaware that I had even touched another's life—to me that's where the hope comes from...that somehow, somewhere I've made a difference."

Though we both like magic words, we agree there aren't any magical solutions. Life is tough. Life happens. There aren't any magic wands to be waved, secret codes to be revealed or incantations to be chanted that can take away the reality of what we must face.

You will not hear magical solutions, religious platitudes, or clichés here. You are too important. Matters are too serious to be treated with an instant answer. The only way to embrace a well-lived life is to walk into it. Stand in the pain, feel the hurt, listen to the adversity. Allow others to encourage and offer hope. Only when you have healed—and I mean healed in the deep places—can you ever begin to rebuild your future.

Risk

At its best, life is a risk. We were not made to experience just the moments of joy and celebration but also the ones of sadness and loss. For life to be complete, we must embrace all of them. I am paraphrasing the words of Carol Mathias in her description of the art of surfing:

"To surf well, you must navigate currents, tide, shore breaking, curls, walls and jellyfish. It is the risk of facing the hazards to find the right conditions to have the perfect ride that is a challenge for both the amateur and competitive surfer. When it all comes together, there is a perfect YES, but in every attempt, there is a gamble. For every day we step outside into the world, rub shoulders with others, and take risks, the challenge is to find which tilted view works, manage those dangerous waves we are not ready for. YES makes it worth the bravery, the commitment, the sacrifice."

When we take away the risk, we rob life of its purpose and vibrancy. I invite you to take a risk now. Walk the "road less travelled" that it will make all of the difference for you.

As the guide to this adventure, let me offer a few brief instructions. There are six sections to the book. To me these mark the movement of life toward wholeness and completion. You will be reading Beginnings, Sources, Entrances and Exits, Wounded Spirits, Healing Souls and Rebirth. You will also see a prayer. These are words I offer on your behalf and mine that we might think of our lives as a living prayer. Every word, action, thought and desire forms a breath of life in this world. At the close of each section, you will see a Reflections page. The goal is simply to capture some of the thoughts that you might carry with you into the next reading.

May your journey begin with hope and excitement as the adventure of your life unfolds in all of its richness and beauty. Celebrate the gift of *you* now.

Beginnings

Prayer for Beginnings

Heavenly Father,

Open the eyes of our hearts that we may look at the roots of our lives with gratitude and honesty. Formed and shaped by influences we did not control nor completely understand, help us to look for your grace that has been ministered to us in silent and hidden ways. Thank you for all of the stories of our beginnings— those that brought us great joy and purpose as well as those that changed the course of who we are in dark and unpredictable ways. Help us to unlock our secrets so that we can release the gift of your grace in a world of broken lives. We ask for courage to live the lives you have given us to live as we are led into the adventure of being your cherished and beloved children.

In Christ's Name,

Amen

Once Upon a Time in Alabama

Every beginning has a story, and mine does as well. I have always been fascinated by "Once upon a time in a far and distant land." Those words hold a bit of magic and fantasy for me. I can envision mystical places and people. My imagination takes me to lands to be conquered and enemies to be overcome. At times, I have wanted those to be the words I could use to describe my life.

Instead, I get to say, "Once upon a time in Alabama about seven miles east of a little crossroads town called Hamilton in a white-washed house along Highway 278, my life began." That just sounds so plain and down to earth in contrast to "...from a far and distant land." Admittedly, few fairy tales actually begin in Alabama, so I don't think there was much chance that my life could have become the material for a fable.

My first memory of home was what I describe as *the old house*. It was on the land when my dad bought the 100 or so acres from his father. Standing on the front porch, you could look out onto fields of corn and cotton. Or you might see pastures with some Hereford cows or mixed-breed pigs. Stay there long enough and a 1951 black GMC pickup might slow down and turn up the graveled drive into our yard.

We don't get to choose the places where we are born. We arrive like a package shipped from God's presence wrapped with innocence, trust and potential. Our places aren't fantasy or exotic destinations. We are born in everyday places like Hamilton, Trenton, Poughkeepsie or Salem. We aren't born into new houses; we are born into relationships that already have a past and a history. Even my family is old; they have a family tree, history and struggle. I just happened to enter a play that was already in progress. No long intermission to announce my birth; just pause for a moment and get back to the routine of work, rest, family, church and struggle.

It isn't the place or the people that determine our greatness. It isn't the success or the failure. It isn't the possessions we accumulate or positions we hold. It is the response we make to life and circumstances of life.

When there is fantasy and mystery, your life holds some mystique. Mine doesn't. I have had a wonderful life. It has been one that moved along a different path than I first expected, but I would never describe it as ordinary.

These are my roots. All of us have them. There is a time, there is a place, and there are people. These are the ones that create our beginning stories.

Life doesn't stay there. It is never static or still but constantly changing and evolving. Time moves forward. Places change. People enter and leave our lives.

I can't sit on the front porch of the old house anymore—it doesn't exist. Fields have disappeared. Pastures are now overgrown. The well-worn paths of childhood can no longer be found.

Every beginning holds a story, and every beginning marks an ending. The life I thought I would live has ended many times. There hasn't been just one or two, but several times when I have had to start over.

This captures the challenge of being alive. There are beginnings where we have people, places and time. There are experiences to be embraced. There are expectations, hopes and dreams. There is reality that hits us head-on. There is the process of rebuilding broken lives and dreams. Some of us can manage this re-creating process pretty well. Some of us don't, and we get stuck.

I am calling this the original YES. It is our life with all of the roots, history and experience. It is my place in this world and the way that I use it. It is my personality, path and pilgrimage. It is me living who I am in consistent and inconsistent ways. It is my energy for being alive. It is me with a divine glimmer shining through and brokenness holding me back. YES is me. It is my gift to the world.

Until my father died, I lived YES, and it was fun: family reunions, church and life in the country. It was energy, joy, playfulness, adventure and safe places. His unexpected illness and death when I was still a boy changed my world in ways I could not anticipate.

We had moved to our new house that my dad had built with the help of family and friends. Old buildings were torn down, lumber salvaged, and work focused on a better place to live. He completed it a few short years before he died.

I guess that was a truth to be discovered. We are always moving between our old houses and our new ones. In the old, there is history, routine and struggle. In our new house there will be opportunity for a better way, promise and hope for a bright future. Or, we try to convince ourselves that it will work in our favor when that day arrives.

When my father died, our family changed as you might expect. My mother became a single parent who had a sixth grade education, a minimum-wage job, and two boys. At age 20, my brother had started college but had to continue without a lot of support. At 9, I engaged in the same activities as before, but with a hole in my heart as large as the universe.

Some of our story we get to write. Some of it is written for us. I had no influence on cancer, surgery or death. I had no say in my mother's remarriage or our life with an alcoholic. And I have sometimes wondered what would have happened if my father had not died.

Yet, out of this tragedy and the chaos that followed our family for years, I grew. There was a move to Mississippi, one back to Alabama and ultimately one to Georgia. There were new schools, teachers and friends. There was change. There was disruption and struggle. With each twist in the road, there was something to be gained and something to be lost.

That is the way it happens: we start, something happens to us, we respond and we move forward. I wish I could say that is the way I did it, but that wouldn't be true. For a long, long time, I was emotionally disabled, wandering around the field in front of our new house—like I did the day my brother told me that our father had died—waiting on someone to come get me and make my world safe again.

Now, I better understand the words of the Apostle Paul when he stated, "When I was a child, I talked like a child, I thought like a child, I reasoned like a child. When I became a man, I put the ways of childhood behind me (I Corinthians 13:11)." There comes a time when you have to move past a child's view of the world and see it through adult eyes.

In looking back on my childhood, I now believe that we sometimes find truth, and sometimes truth finds us. Not the truth of adding one plus one to equal two. Rather, the wisdom that we are being tested by life. We are challenged by events and experiences. We wonder how to survive. We can spend our lives trying to put the pieces back together so that our world looks like it did back in the good ole days, or we can start looking at the pieces and trying to create the best picture we can with what we have to work with. This is the challenge life brings to us.

I invite you to join me on a brief journey—one that I hope will offer you encouragement and hope. I share my story, not to hold it as an example of someone who has done a great job, but one who has tried to do the best that they could; one who has lived with as much courage, faith, and trust as I know how to...one who doesn't see Alabama on the landscape of any fairytale but who believes you can create an intentional purpose and discover a sense of wholeness as you walk the path you have been given, no matter where you were born or what situation you were given as a starting point for life.

Sharing Secrets

"Hello, my name is Randy, and I am a struggler." As though we were a part of an AA support group, I feel the need to confess some of the challenges that mark who I am. I have struggled trying to understand the events in my life, people who have crossed my path, authentic faith and personal truth. As the old saying goes, "I don't have my act together," and the reality is that I probably never will. As Brennan Manning describes, I live as someone whose "cheese is about to fall off of their cracker,"[iii] most of the time.

I do not see this as a sign of weakness. Instead I think it is an indication of strength. It feels good to say, "I don't know, I am not sure or I don't get it." When you don't have an immediate answer, there is openness to learning and growth. New ideas or ways of looking at life serve as possibilities. If I have all of the answers, then I don't need to ask questions or listen to other points of view. That is basically taking an approach that all truth has arrived, and I own it.

I am a seeker. It has taken me a number of years to discover that I face life with curiosity and adventure. This doesn't define who I am as much as it expresses a desire to raise questions, search for information and try to solve problems. There is a thirst for knowledge deep within me. Some of the knowledge that has been the most difficult to gain has been about my own journey. While I am well aware of the events, people and experiences, I have not done as well at making sense of how it all fits together into a cohesive whole.

I am searching now to understand, "Is my life significant; does my life matter?" That may be a concern that surfaces in the aging process. I believe one of the great fears we each have is that we will have lived without making a difference in this world. We lived, we worked, we left, but no one noticed. I am still trying to make peace with this thought.

I am wounded. I believe that when life throws us curveballs, we are touched in the deep places. It isn't just that we lose people or things that we love. That happens to everyone. It is that the wounds go deep, all the way to our souls, and we do not take the depth of the pain seriously. We hear friends say, "You can bounce back or get over it." If it were that simple, we would all be super heroes. We aren't. We are everyday, ordinary people who are walking around with our souls wounded, and we don't know what to do, nor do we know how to fix it or if it can even be repaired.

Some of my wounds are too deep and painful to share with others. To me, this is the grief that cannot be spoken. These are stored away in the holy of holies of my spirit; hidden in the sacred vault of my heart. I have taken a few people there, but most do not even know it exists. I think we all maintain the holy places of brokenness.

Most of the healing that I have experienced has come with the realization that it is okay to hurt. We learn to say that life wasn't fair, didn't work the way I wanted or needed, and has left me with scars. It is in owning the pain that growth occurs.

I am a minister. Before you close the book and turn to some other activity, let me unpack what this statement means to me, because it is critical to everything else I have to offer you for thought. The word *minister* becomes a lightning rod. Some will see it as an opportunity to turn the conversation in a spiritual or religious direction. Others will hear the word and immediately call to mind all of the negative images and stereotypes they have encountered.

I have a reason for sharing this information now. I want to be honest and transparent about my point of view. With more than 40 years of experience, I have observed people try to cope with major struggles in a variety of ways. I have stood with parents as they buried their child, a family whose father was murdered in their front yard, parents and children who have family members who have committed suicide. I have sat with families whose loved ones died by accidents and disease; whose lives were devastated by house fires, tornadoes and flood. I've met with parents dealing with children's sexual orientation; people faced with infidelity and betrayal, surgery and chemotherapy, births of babies, marriages of children, retirements, moves, lost jobs, and a host of other events. All ministers experience similar opportunities.

Through all of these experiences I have watched people try to cope, make life fit, and look for resources of faith that would get them through the dark valley. Some moved into the storm and came out on the other side of it. Some got hit pretty hard and became stuck. They aged but they never moved forward. Emotionally they were locked into a particular time and event.

One lesson I learned from watching others is quite clear. Superficial answers don't work. Telling someone, "It is God's will," is a cheap, irresponsible way to respond to those who are hurting from the loss of a loved one, home or marriage. Slapping a religious bandage on a person's deep wound makes us feel better because we can avoid dealing with our own issues of faith while walking on by the person who has just been annihilated by a tragedy.

I stand in a different place now. I don't think quick-fix answers help others solve major life events, because they didn't work for me. In my mid-40s, a mid-life crisis hit me like a freight train. Unrealistic expectations from the church combined with the lack of a healthy me at the center created a difficult situation. I hit bottom. It was burnout in the purest form. I didn't want to preach. I had nothing to offer; my energy well had hit a drought.

My wife and I went to see a counselor, because I thought the hinges were coming off of my door to sanity. I moaned…I complained. I held one big pity party for myself about how bad life was in the church. At one point, the counselor stated, "Randy, if the church is so painful for you, why don't you leave it?" This question caused me to consider a different fork in the road.

I did leave the organizational role of being a minister for a while, although I never left the spirit of what it means to walk with others in their time of need. I started a business to provide leadership training programs for organizations, and this gave me some distance to look at the role and how I had tried to fill it.

Over time, I began to do some soul work under the guidance of a trusted marriage and family therapist. This required revisiting the pain of my father's death, lack of grieving related to his loss, remarriage of my mother, and struggles with relationships that grew out of these events. I then began to see where I had not set good boundaries. I had taken good care of others but neglected myself.

Slowly, layer upon layer of my life has been peeled back to the point that I now know where my struggles originated. The layers are too numerous and private to share in a public format. Let me summarize that when the roots of pain were revealed, then the path to healing became much clearer.

As I have become healthier as a person, my view of life has changed. I unloaded a whole truck full of unrealistic expectations. There simply wasn't room to hold onto them any longer. I looked at the sources of pain. I looked at the possibilities for growth. I sensed that there was a spirit working within me, even when I couldn't see it, pulling me toward vitality and purpose. I then realized that God's spirit can work in a variety of ways to lead us to wholeness. His truth, eternal principles, worked in the deep places to help me see this wasn't just about me. I wasn't the center of the universe. I wasn't the only person to ever lose a parent, face chaos or struggle with people in the church.

These influences have shaped my concept of what it means to be a minister in a profound way. Being a minister isn't as much a role as it is an outlook on life. I think it is in my spiritual DNA to be one. Maybe the pain has sensitized me, but I believe I have a built-in internal radar that instantly alerts me to hurt in those around me.

I think truth, the awareness of what is really taking place, is critical. It is the knowledge, insight and discernment to see events and people as they really are. Truth must be balanced with compassion. There are wounded spirits all around. They don't need someone to tell them how difficult their condition might be. They need someone to care. Compassion paves the way for healing to take place. It may come in the form of forgiveness, listening, encouragement or accountability. Pain must be acknowledged in the context of genuine interest and concern. Loss, grief and recovery take place as the pain is acknowledged, owned and addressed.

A minister then becomes the facilitator of spiritual healing; a guide to lasting truth, not just popular platitudes borrowed from public opinion, but sacred truths that stand the test of time and speak to the real needs of life. You may share these qualities in a church setting, or you may live them in the world of business, education or health care. The goal of being a minister is to help people find wholeness. It is an on-going call to help others face their pain, search for truth, find paths to healing, claim their wholeness, and live with intention the gifts they have been given.

Being an effective minister means transforming our pain into a useful instrument that allows others to discover "How Can I Live YES in a NO World?" It is never a trophy that you hold up to the world and say, "Look how bad I have had it—I must be the most wounded person of all time." Instead, it stops us in our tracks and makes us realize we are here by grace and grace alone. I didn't create myself, but I have the privilege and opportunity to allow my pain to serve as a source of healing for others.

YES, I am a struggler, a seeker, a wounded person, a guide, and a minister, but I am so much more. I have faced my secrets and discovered in their pain the truth that has led to healing and connects me to others. In the words of Frederick Buechner:

> I believe that by and large the human family all has the same secrets, which are both very telling and very important to tell. They are telling in the sense that they tell what is perhaps the central paradox of our condition—that what we hunger for perhaps more than anything else is to be known in our full humanness, and yet that is often just

what we also fear more than anything else. It is important to tell at least from time to time the secret of who we truly and fully are—even if we tell it only to ourselves—because otherwise we run the risk of losing track of who we truly and fully are, and little by little come to accept instead the highly edited version, which we put forth in hope that the world will find it more acceptable than the real thing.

It is important to tell our secrets too, because it makes it easier that way to see where we have been in our lives and where we are going. It also makes it easier for other people to tell us a secret or two of their own, and exchanges like that have a lot to do with what being a family is all about and what being human is all about.

Finally, I suspect that it is by entering that deep place inside us where our secrets are kept that we come perhaps closer than we do anywhere else to the One who, whether we realize it or not, is of all our secrets the most telling and the most precious we have to tell.[iv]

We all hold secrets. Yet, we tell the same ones. They reveal something of who we are and where the road has taken turns for us. They do not separate us as much as they draw us closer together.

Sacred Stories

Pivotal Moments

My daddy shared this story with me one day. As a little boy, he watched his wonderful momma go through major mental, emotional and physical abuse. They would sneak in his daddy's room late at night, when he was finally passed out, to get money so that they could buy bread to eat. His daddy was mean, and most of the money he worked for went to support his drinking habit. When Daddy got old enough, probably around 12 or 13, he finally stepped in front of his daddy one drunken night, to protect his momma. Yes, that was enough! He told his dad that if he touched his momma, he would show him how it felt!

Yes, from that moment, his momma got the courage and strength to leave her abusive husband. My daddy said that changed his life in the most profound way. He said, "I chose not to be like that man, who was my daddy, but to be just the opposite of him."

I will never forget those words he shared with me, and I do have the most wonderful daddy there is. Yes, he treats my momma like a queen, he waits on her hand and foot, he has the patience of millions of angels, and he has always been the kindest most compassionate man you can imagine.

My daddy and momma graduated from the University of Georgia with honors with no help except from each other. My daddy was a member of Phi Kappa Phi, majored in Forestry but ultimately became a bank president. He is honest, kind, caring, funny, giving, loving and has so many wonderful traits that his daddy did not have! Yes, he chose to be the man he is, and I am thankful for that! He served our country as a pilot in World War II.

I could go on and on about all the things he has done, and my momma too, but I wanted to just say that this pivotal moment in his life was positive. It made him the hard working, kind and caring family man he is. He has a funny sense of humor, too. Whenever any of his children, grandchildren or even great grandchildren does something great, he always says, "It's inherited!"

~**Cindy Edwards**

Adoption and Beyond

The story of adoption does not come down to earth like a capsule with an intended Martha and Jonathan Kent ready to take on the responsibilities of a Kal-El sent from Krypton; nor does it have the nuance, subtlety, and pervasive surreal qualities associated with "Cider House Rules." It may have some qualities of these infused to some degree, but all people have these same common characteristics, which is what makes them appealing. There, you can find some of yourself and be comforted. To understand adoption, you either must be adopted or be part of the family adopting. That too is a fallacy.

Adoption involves identity. For most, identity is established by looking at your most immediate and concrete affiliation with your origin and seeing the common characteristics—but to do that looks only at the concrete and ignores the abstract. My identity—everyone's identity—is determined by my Creator. My

25

identity is in question—or seems to be in question (and seemed to be in question during my childhood and adolescence) because people who are not adopted live under the delusion that blood relations replace the fingerprint of God, and then they project that same thinking onto those of us who are adopted. They do not do this consciously or intentionally; it is just that we all have so much of ourselves invested in our lineage. We think we are family because we have our mother's eyes or our father's sense of humor or our grandparent's temper. While all of this may be true, it does not convey the whole story.

I have a sense of permanence and transience in this world— possibly to a greater degree—than non-adopted people. Who, though, could measure and determine that with any certainty?

In the same way that a challenge presents an opportunity to think creatively and find solutions to problems outside the box, without the foundation of blood relations, I am privileged to look beyond the ties to a specific heritage. If I am to acquire peace, I must dig deeper than the roots of my family tree to find my identity in the creator of the seed itself.

I can put my child to sleep (the one I gave birth to) and think about the parts of him that are the parts of me. My birth mother would be able to look at me and find endearing elements as well, but so could my parents. Without knowing the appearance, talents, and skills of my biological mother or father, I do not have an expectation placed upon me. I do not know where they grew up, where my grandparents came from or live now, how they felt about adoption, whose idea it was, or whether or not they think about me on birthdays, Father's Day, Mother's Day or other holidays. I cannot validate a suspicion I am from good stock or bad stock or determine what I do or do not deserve based on biology. I can appreciate being born in a mysterious way, and I can feel gratitude for knowing my mother and father chose me, raised me to the best of their ability, and love me unconditionally.

My brothers and sister are my siblings, and they are like any other siblings. They aggravate, they love and they support. I was blessed with a mother from Pennsylvania, a father from rural Georgia, and a unique ability to see the world from both sides of the Mason-Dixon Line. Many people have difficulty with that. I do not feel adopted, because I was fortunate to have a family that cares for me. My parents thought of us as part of the family—not adopted kids. My mother said, "When I first held you, you were ours." Even though my two brothers and sister may have come from different ancestry, we were now unified.

Ask me what I know about my birth and I will tell you, "Not one thing." I do know I was born outside marriage to a young woman who wanted me raised Catholic. My ethnicity is Czech-German-Italian, and I was born somewhere in Miami and placed in Catholic charities. I was placed under observation for some time after my birth for a medical anomaly, and then placed in foster care for four to eight weeks.

Adopted people understand and can relate to adoption's realities more so than those who are not. Try thinking about growing up with the following questions coming at you as a 7, 9, or 12-year-old: Is that your real sister? Do you know your real mother? Do you want to find your family? Are you afraid of marrying a relation? Don't you feel lucky to have been chosen for adoption? What generous parents you have!

Maybe that is why those of us who are adopted can find a common friend for support from such destabilizing inquiries that ignore the bounds of common decency. What many adopted people understand is that if I can be chosen, it is because I can be *given away. A person's value appears to be negotiable. All this happens before you can understand yourself, the world, or even the most basic premise behind "The Lion King." The circle of life has been altered—maybe not for a negative or a positive reason—but because circumstances, or my Creator, deemed it so.*

People who adopt make considerations regarding the child when choice provides that option. Potential adoptive parents may consider the health of the biological parents, the gender of the child, the length of time the child spends in foster care, the trauma history from conception on, and the more superficial characteristics like eye color, hair color, dental history, height, skills, talents, and achievement. One of the coolest things ever is being able to see someone who looks like you. I have not yet had that (my son looks like his father). I may be able to one day see it in his children.

In a fair and secure world, all adoptees would have parents who put forth the great effort necessary to understand adoption and realize the fundamental truth—that adoption means belonging rather than ownership. An adopted person may find as much meaning in not being related to as in being a permanent part of the family. Potential parents would know about the evolution of adoption practices through the centuries. They would know that nothing can be predicted, even with meticulous planning. They would struggle as biological parents do, with Kahlil Gibran's message:

Your children are not your children.
They are the sons and daughters of Life's longing for itself.
They come through you but not from you,
and though they are with you yet they belong not to you.[v]

I grew up with the security of being in a family—an imperfect one in some ways—but an especially caring family where my Mom and Dad sacrificed to provide me and my siblings with opportunities to make the most of our lives. When I wanted to play an instrument, they came up with the $150 for a used flute (that was a lot of money for one child back then). I was part of an Air Force family where I developed and cherished friendships with my sister, my friends and through my church. I still call on my brothers, sister, and parents when I need help now, and they reciprocate. We are a family like most families— we argue, support and love one another.

I do not like to give out information about myself in my role as a counselor, because the focus is on the client. But if someone is struggling with adoption, and I think it will help him move toward treatment goals, I share that my experience with adoption is my own and has developed (and continues to grow and evolve) over my lifetime. Sometimes, just allowing the client to know I am adopted helps improve her comfort with processing the experience. Being able to identify with others—to realize we are not the only ones—helps soothe the distress of not knowing. We have our own blank slate to paint, but all around us, there are others too who have a world to fill with the experiences our Creator has blessed us with.

~Karen Annette Jones Richardson

You Will Go

Sometimes I think we experience a YES, and at the time are not aware of the impact that it will have on our lives. For me an important YES came at the end of my high school career. My dad was a very firm believer in education. He had only a high school education, but always wanted a college education for my sister and me. When I graduated from high school, his resounding "Yes, you can and will go to college," was loud and clear. At the time I didn't put a lot of stock in that YES—I just went because my dad said, "Yes, you can...yes, you will... yes, this is something I want you to do." My dad did the same thing with my husband three years later when he was thinking of dropping out of college. I can still hear him, "Son, what is the problem? Yes, you need an education. Yes, I will help you finish school. Yes, I will give you $10 a week for gas".

My dad didn't get to live to see us graduate. He passed away in June before my husband graduated in August. But when I graduated, I mouthed to the sky, "Yes, Daddy, I did it". This past May I retired from 30 years of teaching, thanks to an important YES in my life. As I left school for the last time that day in May, I mouthed to the sky, "Thank you, Daddy, for 30 wonderful years that would have never happened without your "Yes, you will go to college!"

    ~Dianne Junkins Gregg

Reflections

Our beginnings mark the starting line for our walk through life. They do not dictate who we will become or what we will achieve. Instead, these first memories provide inspiration for the person we want to become.

From this start, some will dream of distant places and significant goals that will challenge them to reach higher or further than ever imagined. For others, the desire forms to make a difference through service and compassionate acts of kindness.

You don't have to be born into a great family or in a wonderful place. We are born into everyday families in ordinary locations. It isn't the start that makes you who you are. It is what is born in your heart to become—the person you believe you were called to be. Family and friends help, but to a large degree greatness depends upon you. And greatness isn't about the money you accumulate, titles you hold, or positions you achieve. It is the honesty, transparency, and openness you practice as you face the challenges, walk into the adversity, and learn the deeper lessons of life along this journey with others. Do you believe you are a wonderful, talented, compassionate gift to the world? If that is what you believe, then that is who you will become.

In truth, we don't make one beginning; we make many beginnings over and over again. With each new person, relationship, or event, we go about transforming ourselves into someone that is like the old but totally different at the same time. We take with us all of the memories and pain and secrets.

31

Your life becomes a never-ending story of re-inventing yourself to meet the challenges of new and different needs or situations.

Beginnings mark where our journey started, not how it will end. Accept them with gratitude. Embrace the opportunity...enjoy the gift of you.

Sources

Prayer for Sources

Heavenly Father,

As the creator of all life, O' God, we thank you for the many words, stories, memories and beliefs that have influenced our growth and development. We have not always received what we thought that we needed. Instead, the good words—ones of hope, love, and forgiveness— have come to us in unexpected and surprising ways.

May we hear your call to continue the journey of discovery as we revisit stories and memories from long ago that still linger on the edges of our souls. Help us to hear them not through the ears of our weariness but through the heart of grace that you give to each of us.

Thank you for the opportunity to open up old doors that we might discern new truths that will lead us to a better day.

In Christ's Name,

Amen

Buying Puzzles

In the movie "Forrest Gump," Forrest states, "My Momma always said life is like a box of chocolates; you never know what you are going to get."[vi]

I do believe our journey here is filled with many surprises, but for me it is more like a jigsaw puzzle. You buy one based upon the picture on the cover, expecting to put those pieces together to recreate the image on the outside of the box. But life tends to shuffle the pieces around some so that the picture you thought you were going to create changes.

As a child growing up, I thought I would always live along Highway 278 seven miles east of Hamilton, Ala. My view of the future included becoming a farmer or teacher. At least that is what was revealed as a vocation during a summer program at the Hamilton United Methodist Church that I attended with some of my cousins. My puzzle would have been one of living close to family, growing up and old near those I knew, and spending time in the country. I could only imagine living in the same house, being with the same family and friends, going to the same church and working in the same community.

One day the words changed, and so did the pieces of the puzzle. *Death* entered my vocabulary. Nine-year-old boys aren't supposed to bury their fathers, but they do. With it, came *loss* and *grief.* My sense of family changed. My father left way too soon. My mother moved into survival mode. My brother faced his own responsibilities, and I was left to figure out how to put the pieces together on my own.

Other uninvited words entered my world that weren't in my original picture. I had known *stability, protection* and *support.* These were exchanged for *uncertainty, doubt* and *hurt.*

A brief year or so later, mother began to date a man she met through her work. He was different. He didn't talk, act or behave like my dad. He drank alcohol, slurred words and claimed my mother's attention. He wanted to join our family, and I said, "No," but that didn't matter.

We moved. There were fights. There were nights alone.

Words couldn't express all of the memories. With them came new beliefs about me and my world. I didn't seem to be important to anyone. I was there. I was loved. They were good people, but their attention was turned in another direction. I wandered around always as a good person. This I had learned—good people don't cause problems. When you cause problems, people get upset, and being upset becomes an argument or fight. Furniture gets thrown around; threats are made; and everyday becomes one moment of turmoil after another.

With beliefs, I formed expectations of how life would go. I imagined life back on our farm with adventures and happy experiences. So my imagination was a means of escape. I could play, even alone, and escape the realities of a dysfunctional family. I would imagine what I would do if this event took place or another course of action occurred.

As an adult, it has been interesting to go back and unpack some of the words, memories and expectations. The process has been one that has brought closure and healing.

Words, memories, beliefs and expectations are the building blocks of our lives. We expect to get one life. That is the picture on the cover that we buy. It may be one of a long and lasting marriage. It may be success at work and all of the benefits of a career with one employer. It may be the birth of children and their growth throughout life. It may be a new home in a different city.

All of us are buying puzzles. We look at this box called life and say, "I am buying this picture right here. This is the one I want." With that emotional commitment, we focus all of our expectations on the pieces falling into place in a seamless and automatic process. When things don't come together as planned, we get lost and confused. We bought one picture but receive the pieces for a different one altogether.

Where I see people often struggle is at the point of expectations. When our hopes are not realized, we get disillusioned with ourselves, our lives and God. This leaves us sitting on the floor, looking at the box and muttering to ourselves, "This isn't the puzzle I bought." I don't think many people ever live the lives they thought they would be living.

A Question Visits

Late one afternoon a "question" walked up to the front porch of my life, sat down in a rocking chair, and looked at me. When it began to speak, I immediately recognized the voice. I knew it was one that had whispered quietly to me on many occasions over the years...at least that is how it felt. It seemed as though I was finally meeting someone whom I had known for a long time.

I would like to say that *I* found the *question*. It would be more accurate to say the *question* found *me*. I was in the middle of a conversation with my wife and a friend about different options and actions I could take. It was a reflective discussion about self-understanding, blockages and personal growth. In one exchange, the question popped up, and there it was. I had searched for it for years, and at that moment, it simply walked into the room without any fanfare at all. I didn't need an introduction; at each step in my journey the question had walked with me. It was with me at 9 when my father died, and I struggled with grief, loss and pain. It lived with me when my mother married an alcoholic two years later, and I was often left alone. It traveled with me when our family began a series of chaotic moves in an effort to find stability.

Unfortunately, I was too young to understand and too busy just trying to survive. I didn't have the time, nor was I mature enough to appreciate what was being asked of me. As if looking at a Norman Rockwell painting, I was aware of a face in the background of a picture, but I never got to know it very well.

That is how I related to this familiar, and yet mysterious, travel companion.

Now that we were ready to talk, I was a little nervous, yet excited. So, we rocked, and the question spoke, "Do you know what I have come to ask of you?" Without a lot of thought or reflection, I answered. When I began to speak, I didn't think about education, training, experience or achievements. Instead, the words seemed to roll off of my tongue spontaneously, giving voice to a question that had resided deep down in the recesses of my heart and spirit for a very long time. Once voiced, it was truly a cathartic moment for me, one that I realized I had needed for quite some time, "How Can I Live YES in a NO World?"

I do not want to suggest that in that moment I located the secret code that can transform adversity into happiness. Instead, I walk on a path that I hope leads to contentment. It is a well-worn walkway, because I think everyone searches for the same destination, and yet, we often put on our equipment and uniforms only to stand on the sidelines of life waiting...waiting while more intelligent, talented, gifted or blessed people seem to play the game called *Life*. At least this is what we convince ourselves of as we consciously or subconsciously attempt to find our place in this world, among the superficial reading of magazines, newspapers and current events. Sadly, when we compare our lives to others, we never feel adequate.

That is why the question becomes so important. Life isn't about appearances. Life isn't about being the best, brightest or most influential. It isn't about setbacks, disappointments or struggles. To me, it is about discovering *your* question. Or, maybe I should say, letting your question discover *you*.

The Teacher Arrives

My lifelong travel companion transformed from being a question to being my teacher. As I did a quick review of my life in light of the question, layer upon layer of insight began to emerge. The answers I thought I knew were revisited and reframed. I saw people and experiences in a new light. I looked at myself from a different perspective.

Was it uncomfortable to do this? Yes! Without a doubt, I can say it was not easy. My life, my stories and my beliefs were so entrenched in my memory that I had developed a personal movie of my life. I had a highlight reel that I played on demand to illustrate all of the bad, ugly and pain. It might as well have been titled "My Tough Life and All of the Bad Things that Have Happened to Me."

For many years, I could retell the story of my life to others and put a slant on it about the sadness and pain. Doing this allowed me to create one continuous pity party for myself. I viewed my experiences as though I was the victim of some random sequence of events.

When my question stopped by for a visit, something changed. Suddenly, all of the major events in my life took on a new appearance. I could see that with every setback I had faced, YES had been present. Sometimes the YES came from within me as I had worked through difficult situations or challenges. Sometimes the YES came through the support and encouragement of others. This was not easy to admit. I wanted to hold onto the pain, pity and beliefs that had been engrained in my story for years. Yet with YES, there wasn't just the story of struggle; now there was hope, encouragement, support and recovery. I could feel a whole new energy about life.

41

When the question arrived, I was no longer the victim. It didn't allow me to be. Rather, I could see a common thread woven through every stage of my life. It was an eye-opening moment in time for me. I began to see applications of the message to many points of adversity:

How can you face the death of a loved one and learn to live again?

How can you lose your job and rebuild your future?

How do you face cancer and live with purpose?

How do you hear the words, "I don't love you anymore," and find a way to live again?

With time I have learned it is a very basic question, yet it has stretched me in many ways. For I have come to find that this is the question I believe *my* life has called *me* to answer.

The Truth Emerges

As my question and I visited together, something changed. It then dawned on me—*I* was the change. I had come home to my life, and, for the first time, I felt comfortable being there. It was my place. It belonged to me. I was thrilled to celebrate being *me*. I could finally embrace all of the parts; the broken and the whole ones. I was able to look at my life with a sense of appreciation and affirmation. There wasn't any need to blame. It didn't matter what people had or had not done. All guilt was removed. Peace washed over me as though I was lying on the beach waiting for the next wave to arrive.

For some people, these thoughts will seem too peculiar, and the words will fall on deaf ears. For most though, I hope it will make perfect sense because it is a basic belief, a simple truth: Most of us are not at home with ourselves, and we don't know it, or it scares us to death.

We haven't found peace in being who we are in this world. The events, experiences and people are more like a jigsaw puzzle scattered on the floor rather than a roadmap we can hold in our hands. To compare it to a roadmap assumes that we know the destination, that there is a clear direction, and that the way to get there is explicit and defined.

I believe that everyone's life has a purpose. Unfortunately, there are many voices out there who claim to have the answer. Instead of clarity though, their voices become a sea of noise and dissonance, often making answers harder to hear. Religious leaders will often speak with loud, powerful voices that say, "God has a purpose for your life." Business leaders will shout, "Find meaning in your work." Non-profit organizations will suggest "Help others by donating your time and money." Despite all of these "answers," we continuously flounder, fumble and fall more than we walk with any sense of confidence.

In desperation, we turn to one new adventure or relationship after another. It may be that we frequent the "shopping mall of life," hoping we can find a meaningful purpose. We look into each face in the crowd, hoping we will see a familiar one who will give us the love and affirmation we need. Or we stop in every store, trying to buy that one thing that will bring peace and contentment. Unfortunately, we go home with our hands empty.

We hold on to our pain, but don't know what to do with it. Do we hang it around our neck like some giant albatross that goes with us wherever we go? Or do we put it in a backpack, hoping we can hide it out of sight as we struggle under the increasing weight of the hurt? We keep hoping we can discover the secret code, find a magical formula, or receive the divine revelation that will remove all of the confusion and doubt. Deep down we know it doesn't exist, but that doesn't stop us from glancing around for a magic wand every now and then.

I know all of these frustrations. I share them. I have lived them. I have experienced them first-hand, but the day my question found me, so did a simple truth: You Can Live YES in a NO World.

Reflections about the Visit

This truth didn't just walk into my world and introduce itself one day. This has been the ongoing challenge of life itself. How do you do it? When things fall apart, how do you live YES? When you hurt, how do you want YES? When you struggle, how do you create YES? When you want to become healthier, how do you practice YES?

Rather than live in the pain, complain about how unfair events that happen are, or stay paralyzed from taking action, I want to suggest that there is another way. It takes more time. It requires courage, openness and transparency. It is the path to learning and growth.

Until you hear the question, I don't think you will ever discover the truth. Finding it is only the beginning of the journey. You must then face the struggle of living the truth in every dimension of life. When your truth finds you, the desire to live it every moment of your life floods your soul with awareness, need and possibilities. This discovery of your truth creates an internal alignment of passion, purpose and mission that becomes your power for being alive. This is what I am calling your YES for life.

This book is intended to offer you a different way of looking at this process. I deliberately selected YES and NO as the doorway to understanding. These are basic words with five letters total. Yet, these two become the gatekeepers to your experience. Use them carefully and things work well. Ignore them and you find a world of heartache.

Everyone holds expectations of how good, perfect and wonderful life will be. Yet, reality often hits us like a truck. This is what I am calling your NO for life. It is the external and internal resistance we face as we seek to live with intention. So, what do you do then? This is where we all live. We look for solutions to the illusions, false expectations and dilemmas we face.

I am not suggesting a band-aid solution to your struggles. I don't think quick fixes work in the long term. Instead, I recommend that you take an honest look at your life and learn from the pain, mistakes and setbacks. What better source of learning can there be than *you*?

I invite you now to walk with me for a little while as we look at this thing called *life* and see what we can learn along the way.

In Search of Our Missing Words

Life Puzzles

Words shape our lives. If the right words are in place, we do well. If the right words are not in place, we search for them all of our lives.

I believe each of us receives a core crossword puzzle to solve. It goes to the depth of our soul and spirit. It relates to acceptance, affirmation, value and respect. It has to be finished by us alone, though others can help. When done, we discover the code for contentment with who we are as a person. With these key messages in place, our lives are not as much of a puzzle. We have words that go down that gives us security and strength. Our words across empower us to connect with others and develop meaningful relationships. We have the vertical and horizontal dimensions of life in place.

For this reason, I believe our search for meaning and purpose begins at a basic level. It starts with words. Those little boxes of information that we package with emotion, seal with tone and send out with urgency carry the secret code to our existence. It seems that there are some empty slots at the core that when filled with the right words become the "atomic energy for life." We can move forward with a sense of completion. It is having the sense of "I have what I need." We have the right material for building a solid foundation of affirmation, security and confidence. We can move forward with confidence to discover our sense of self, develop personal power, and find our place in this world.

Yet, all words are not created equal. There are big words and small ones. There are strong ones and weak ones. Some are used so often they become meaningless and no longer hold any value. We use the word *love* to describe our favorite food, music or pastime, so that when we share it with someone special, it has lost some of its punch. Our search starts with finding the right people who can provide us with the words we need to do well in life.

I think we need to use stronger words. We need to send powerful messages to our children with words and actions that clearly communicate critical information. They need to hear loud and clear that they are loved, wanted and protected. If we can't do it, then we need to find people who can. This may include grandparents, teachers, coaches, ministers or others who can inspire and encourage their growth.

YES and NO

I discovered the power of YES and NO by accident. While reflecting on life one day, I wrote, "I like the word YES. It opens doors, creates opportunities and releases energy into the world. With this one word you can change the course of your life."

When I shared this thought with my friend Mary Ann Prior, she quickly responded, "Randy, there is a story I want you to hear." I will let her tell it in her words now.

> *Twelve years ago I gave birth to my last son, making a family of four children. Daniel was just a few weeks old, born in late August. School had already started and the chaos of "routine" had begun ... It was 4 o'clock on this*

48

particular afternoon. The doorbell rang, and it was Ms. Hunter. The children (then ages 9, 6, 5 and newborn) were running around, and the dog got loose and the doorbell rang. I answered the door and must have looked a sight. She quietly came and asked to hold Daniel. I was encouraged to sit quietly too. She began rocking him on her knees looking right at him... did I mention it was his fussy time of day? He was crying and she began saying/chanting "yes" over and over and over. It continued until I was a bit uncomfortable, and she never once looked my way.... over and over..."yes, yes, yes, yes, yes..."oh dear...

Five minutes passed, and I thought I would get my house back "together." I caught the dog, got the kids settled, probably started dinner, and all the while, "yes, yes, yes, yes..." Finally I sat back down. Daniel was quiet, the house still, and she stopped, looked at me and said, "He will hear enough NO in life. I wanted to start him with YES." This story has stayed with me for many reasons. It took courage to do that—to knock and to ask for Daniel. It took time, which no one has. It took wisdom (although not much) to see a young mom in distress. It took love to send a blessing through touch, time and prayer. What a blessing we can be to each other, if only we had her courage, time and wisdom. I try to remember that we fall short on many things, but if willing, God provides it all.

It helps to know a little information about Ms. Hunter. She died in 2010 at the age of 103. She was approximately 91 when she visited Mary Ann on this particular afternoon. Ms. Hunter was a kind and lovely individual who lived out her faith in quiet ways every day.

Later, I thought about the tension in two small words. There are voices that will speak YES to you while others will speak NO. Hopefully, you will hear more positive words than negative ones, but you can't be certain if that will take place or not.

I could also see how instrumental others can be in offering encouragement and strength. I first heard the *words* that Ms. Hunter spoke to Daniel. How calming her demeanor must have been in helping him settle down at a fussy time of day. I wondered what an impact Ms. Hunter's presence was for Mary Ann. She didn't judge the condition of Mary Ann's house nor her parenting skills. She entered into all the activity and chose the most urgent need of all as her focus. When someone takes time to walk into your world, push aside any resistance, and sit with you until the problem is solved, that is a powerful form of encouragement. I don't know if she was trying to be a prophet or not, but I think she was on target. There will be plenty of NOs in life. It is the responsibility of those who love us to speak with insight the right NO and the right YES at the best time.

Sometimes parents and family do a really good job of saying YES, and sometimes they miss the mark altogether. This may be due to generational factors, family dynamics, or personal comfort. I don't know all of the reasons this doesn't take place. I just know many people have shared with me the void they feel from not hearing these simple words from the people who mattered to them.

Missing Words

I polled a group of friends. I asked them a question, "What is one word that you wish you could have heard from parents or significant people in your life when you were growing up as a child?" The response was quick and spontaneous. I was surprised at how freely individuals shared their struggle with simple words:

- *Yes, you are loved. No, you cannot move out at 15. Yes, no matter how I feel about your other parent, we love you. These are words I really wished I had heard growing up.*
- *Yes, you are smart/ NOT smart; nice/ NOT nice. Yes, you can succeed/ NOT succeed. Whatever the situation, I wish there would have been more honesty and truth in the words of my mentors. So often, we try to keep our children from the truth to protect them, but in the long run, it only makes reality more difficult as adults.*
- *Yes, you are loved. I know it is hard to imagine, but those are words I cannot remember hearing from my parents. They passed away without me hearing them. Although I did say those words to them, for some reason they could not say them to me. I do not remember them saying these words to each other. So I did not hear them in my household growing up. I have always tried to make it known to our children. Yes, I love you in words and actions. I am 59 years old, and you know it still hurts, but I have tried to reason it out over the years and make sense of it.*

- *I am almost 72 years old, and when we were growing up I cannot remember ever hearing the words "I love you" from our parents. They were not bad parents, but for some reason these words were never said!*
- *Yes, you have a right to feel the way you do and hold the opinions that you have. No, you may not always be right, but you will learn from your mistakes and grow from them. But yes, your thoughts and feelings do count.*

All of these responses came from responsible adults. These are mature people who have families and function well in life. Yet, even as adults there are gaps. We don't always hear YES from the people closest to us. The words are easy to say and take very little effort. Yet, they are missing in the vocabulary of some families.

Ingers

I knew this concept was a familiar one, because I had heard it in different forms for many years. In fact, our daughters had helped me see it when they were growing up. When both of our children were very young, my wife, Dianne, and I learned many lessons from them.

An episode one Sunday gave this message new meaning. Frequently, I retreated to my study on Sunday afternoons to research and prepare for my next presentation. At the time, this seemed like the most important task in the world. So I'd gone into my office and closed the door that day to get some much needed privacy. Before long, Laura, our youngest daughter, discovered I was missing, and she made it her personal mission to find me. Soon she discovered I was in the office and began to knock on the door. Over and over again, she knocked. I would tell her, "Give me a few minutes and I will be through with my work. Then I will come out and play with you." I was actually thinking that she would give up and stop.

Her persistence continued until I heard her say, "Daddy, see my ingers, Daddy, see my ingers?" There sticking under the door and wiggling as fast as she could make them move were the short little fingers of a 4-year-old girl. She didn't know about the research and didn't care about the presentation. She just wanted some time with her daddy. At some level, she needed to hear the word YES.

"See my ingers, Daddy, see my ingers," became a communication signal within our family. These words became our code for marking what we believed to be special moments for our children.

Over the years, I have watched those ingers grow. They were waving at my wife and me when both of our teenage daughters climbed the super, duper, giant, one-of-a-kind waterslide at the amusement park. There they stood high on the platform looking closely to see if we were watching. I heard the unspoken message, "See my ingers, Daddy, see my ingers" as they waved to us below.

I thought of these words when Laura received her driver's license. We bought her a used Honda Accord. It was a good and reliable car for a 16-year-old. The first time she headed out on her own, she backed out of the driveway, turned toward town, beeped the horn twice, and then waved out of the driver's side window. I heard the message loud and clear, "See my ingers, Daddy, see my ingers?"

I saw them when our daughter Lindsay married her husband, Todd. The wedding was beautiful. Following the reception, she and Todd climbed into the limousine to leave. As the car pulled away, Lindsay turned for a brief moment, looked out the back window and waved. I heard the message again, "See my ingers, Daddy, see my ingers?"

There have been so many "see my ingers" moments now that we can look back on—special times when one of our girls wanted to know if we were paying attention. I can't say we caught every one as well as we could, but we have tried to make sure our girls heard one word loud and clear as a consistent message. And that word is YES.

This communication signal helped us as parents realize that at a very deep level our children needed to hear one word. They needed to hear YES—Yes, you are loved...Yes, you are important...Yes, your mother and I are paying attention to your life...Yes, we love you unconditionally.

Empty Places

Having worked with a number of people over the years as they have processed major life events and searched for ways to start over again, I am convinced now, more than ever, that YES is the one word we really want to hear. We need to hear that we are affirmed as a person of value and worth. We want to know we are loved by those we consider most important. We seek to give ourselves permission to live the life we believe we have been called to embrace.

This need for words doesn't take place just at the beginning of life. A void occurs at each major life moment. A person is abused as a child, and they feel violated. They want to hear, "I am sorry that was inappropriate." Or, your soul mate one day says, "I don't love you anymore." You begin to question your worth and value as a person. A loved one dies and you wonder, "Where is God now?"

If these valued messages are not heard or if they are left unspoken, the underlying need travels with us for years. We go into marriages hoping the partner will speak what we want to hear, and we spend an inordinate amount of life energy trying to get them to say it. Or, we attempt one venture after another striving to fill the empty places in our hearts.

These are small words. In some cases, they could be uttered in just a few seconds. They don't require a lot of energy or time, yet they mean so much to the people around us. It isn't just the words though. We need to hear them spoken by the right person. They need to come from a parent, our spouse, a significant person in our lives or the person we long to connect with.

The simple words and messages that have been discussed here are the foundational ones of life. These basic messages give us our sense of security, affection and value in our self as a person. When the adults in our world communicate them in word and action we can develop an internal sense of confidence that our needs are met and life is good. With these values in place, we can move forward looking for opportunities to use our best skills, talents and abilities to shape the world around us.

When the adults in our world do not let us know that we are loved, wanted or valued, it creates a void that we continue to seek to fill for the rest of our days. We look into the face of every friend, neighbor, co-worker, significant other and relative hoping we will hear the unspoken words and missing messages. We listen to every word uttered hoping that the words we long to hear will be spoken. This sets us up for unending disappointment and pain. Relationships are then built on a faulty foundation and ultimately fail to support long-term health or well-being.

In the following pages, I want to explore the word *YES*. I want to relate it to some of the ways we experience affirmation, permission and encouragement. Yet, there is another side to this word. Sometimes we want YES and get it, but pain comes with it.

What does this have to do with "How Can I Live YES in a NO World?" To me, life is tough on the good days. It takes courage to face the challenges and adversity that comes our way. It takes even more courage to recreate your life after you have been knocked off the highway, through the ditch, and over the cliff. When adversity strikes, we are rocked to the core. Every root is stretched. Every belief challenged. Weaknesses are revealed. Pat answers do not work. We need a more grounded and consistent solution.

For these reasons, I believe YES is the word we need to hear. Sometimes it comes to us from others. Sometimes we must voice the word and speak it to ourselves. It is an ongoing search of the human spirit to hear the words that will give us the affirmation we need in the depths of our being. This becomes the foundation of trust we need for rebuilding and recreating our lives again over and over again.

Also, I think we use our words as the building blocks of life. We experience life. We feel the emotions of these moments. Through these moments we use our words to form stories. Our stories become memories. Our memories create our beliefs. Our beliefs shape our expectations. Suddenly small insignificant words become the telltale sign of where a person has been shaped, encouraged, discouraged, hurt, pained, celebrated or affirmed. The road map of where we were touched and how we have been influenced appears as clear as can be.

Visiting the Hall of Fame

A Street Called Remember

With our words, we express emotions, describe experiences and discuss what is taking place in our world. We pull words together to form a larger unit of thought...stories. These become the vehicles I use for describing how the world has treated me.

Often, I walk down Memory Lane, the place where all of the people, emotions, events and experiences related to me, reside. These moments of life play and rewind over and over again. In some ways, they are as much alive today as the moment I experienced them. Name a place, push a button, and a movie plays in my memory of exactly what took place at a particular moment in time.

See the large white wooden building beside the highway? That is Sugar Bend Elementary School. It was a satellite school for Marion County, Ala. back in the 40s, 50s and 60s. My first six years of education took place in those three rooms. Ms. Sanderson, Ms. Shotts and Ms. Hamilton were all my teachers and a major source of influence on me. It was in that building that I learned the basics of reading, writing, math and life.

I learned to play with others when we'd go outside to the yard behind the school during lunch and recess. There wasn't any playground equipment, so we made up our own games. One autumn we took large pieces of scrap wood that were stored under the school and built a fort. It was amazing. We could hide, play and create imaginary places behind the walls we built. A new boy came to our school one day, and during recess he came to play with us, but we wouldn't let him. Ms. Hamilton soon discovered what we were up to and gave us an ultimatum, "Let him play or tear down the fort, now." We let him play. From this, I learned we build physical walls, but we sometimes build emotional ones as well.

On my walk down Memory Lane, there are houses, people, experiences and emotions. I can point to a building, and suddenly all of the people related to it come to life again. In a sense, I think our memory becomes our personal *hall of fame*, a place where all our good and not-so-good moments live.

I cannot share all of my memories with you. It would take too much time and it would be a little boring. I can say that I don't think you store memories away without energy being attached to them. That is the reason that when you walk down Memory Lane some of the events still living there call out your name. These are the significant ones that you associate strong positive or negative emotions with. Each one is deposited into our memory bank account as a credit or debit. A *credit* simply means this was a positive experience, and I have good thoughts or feelings connected with it. A *debit* means it was an event that left an emotional mark on my life, and I have not finished processing it yet.

It is easy to see how this transaction takes place. In response to the poll I mentioned in the last chapter, I received one person's experience about longing to hear specific words from a parent. It is brief, but it is very moving in what it conveys.

> *I had never heard my Father say the words, "I love you." Mother said it freely as we kissed her goodbye, but Daddy only grunted when kissed and told "I love you." One day, in front of my niece—she was probably about 14 years old at the time—I said, "I am afraid I will never hear the words from him before he dies."*

> *The next Sunday when my niece started to leave, she kissed her Granddad and said, "I love you." He gave his usual grunt to which she replied, "What do you say?"*

He said, "What?" She said, "I love you, now what do you say to me?"

He actually said, "Thank you."

She said, "No, you say I love you too."

He said, "You know I love you."

She said, "Well say it then."

He said, "Well, I love you too."

She said, "Okay, now don't forget it."

I cried all the way home because she had done at 14 what I hadn't been able to do at 40! The next Sunday when I kissed Daddy goodbye I said, "I love you." I got the grunt again, and I said, "I thought Phyllis taught you what to say back when someone says they love you."
He said, "Oh, I love you too."

Once again I cried all the way home, because I had heard my father actually say the words. He never said them again, and I never prompted him again either, but I had heard them once. I did know that he loved me as much as he was capable of loving, but I do cherish having heard him say the words, and I'm grateful to my niece for being practical enough to teach him.

It took me a long time to understand (and forgive) that he couldn't give to me what he didn't know how to give. I realized he had never received it himself. Hard times didn't have very much softness for children, so he never learned "I love you...good job...way to go" or "I'm proud of you." This was his loss and mine as well.

This is a story that has traveled year after year throughout every family gathering and frequently surfaced during moments of reflection. A Sunday afternoon tradition was transformed when her father said he loved her. In that instant the memory moved from being a debit to one of being a credit.

Our life seems to consist of a series of stories. We are born. We have a family. We go to school. We make decisions. We live. We move. We work. We weave all of the moments, hours and experiences together into a consistent picture that we call our lives.

Drawing a Picture

In the collection of our memories, we are trying to create a picture of wholeness. Sometimes we do a really good job of it. Like when leaves fall from the tree, and we rake them up, put them in one nice pile and call this a moment in life. We take a mental and emotional picture of this to store it away for future reference as we grow older. Life feels good, organized, and there seems to be an order to who we are.

Other times the leaves fall, we rake them up, we put them in a pile and the wind blows through sending our well organized collection all over the yard and into the street. You can't find the pieces. Some are there, while others are missing. You feel the incompletion and live with it every second of your life.

When Dianne and I lived in Elizabethtown, Ky., we resided in a brick house on a hill. Backing up to our house, was a home owned by a retired military officer and his wife. My yard usually stayed a little untended, and his yard was meticulously groomed by his wife. One fall, I decided I would do a better job in caring for my yard, so as the leaves fell, I raked them up.

Then I carried them one load at a time to the side street that was beside our two homes and dumped them on the curb for the city to pick up. My yard looked great! It was clean and neat for the first time in a long time.

Then high winds moved into the area and scattered my neat pile of leaves downhill into the meticulously groomed yard of my neighbor. The next day he came for a visit and let me know how bothered he was by this event. Our conversation was both pleasant and strained. I thought it odd that during the year or so we had lived near each other, we had never talked much about anything. But when the wind relocated the leaves, there suddenly was a need to communicate.

We engaged in a lengthy and heated conversation. He recommended that I spend a large portion of the day raking up the leaves for his wife. I suggested this was not an option I was going to pursue. And I stored away a memory from this exchange that has stayed with me for many years.

Purpose of Stories

So, how do stories figure into our growth and development as a person? I don't know all of the answers to this question. Yet, I have spent a lot of time telling and retelling the events or experiences of my life to try to make sense of who I am in this world. From this practice, I think I have gained some insight on what makes me tick. With time and reflection, I have a few ideas to offer for your consideration.

I see stories as small packages of life that we have neatly boxed and wrapped up. It gives us a way of keeping events in bite-size chunks. I can pull out one tiny container rather than open up the whole closet. These small packages are vehicles for me to use to introduce the people and events that have shaped me personally. I often consider our lives to be something like a stage production. There are characters, events and twists in the play. Some of the drama took place in the past. Some of it is taking place now. When we talk about the people in our lives, we are letting others see some of the characters and conversations that have shaped the person we are today.

If I mention the name *Aunt Madie*, that would have very little meaning to most people. To me she is a great aunt that stepped into my world the summer my father was sick and died. She and her husband were the sole source of security for me at a very uncertain time in my life. In just a couple of sentences, I have introduced you to one of the most significant people in my whole life.

I can also use my stories to help people understand how YES and NO have been factors to me. YES was the early years of life before there was sickness and death. These were times spent with my family, playing in the woods, running up and down the creek bank and generally being a little boy.

The NO entered unexpectedly when my father's sickness and death turned my YES world upside down. NO moved from being an unknown word to a daily experience as childhood became riddled with adult responsibilities—mother's remarriage, stepfather's alcoholism, moves, and lots of uncertainty then followed.

My stories are also indicators of where life has become bonded for me. Like a candle dripping hot wax on a cloth, there are places in my journey where the heat of life events has burned scars and melted moments into one indiscernible piece of fabric. I cannot pull apart any piece without destroying the integrity of the whole.

Stories have helped me organize my life. I have a number of geographical locations in my walk through this world, and each one carries a whole collection of stories. Like, "Do you remember the time we tried to find Huber's Orchard in Indiana and drove for 30 minutes in the wrong direction?"

This leads me to another truth that I have learned about our life stories. Each one goes through an interpretation process. We interpret the details of each one in a way that gives it the emotional slant we want others to perceive about our life. The next phase of life came when my mother, stepfather and I moved to Fulton, Miss. These are the times I remember hardship, abandonment and uncertainty. I was alone a lot. So, these memories carry pain with them— emotional uncertainty that didn't have to take place, but did. The time I was left alone to run a restaurant for three hours while my mother went to bail my stepfather out of jail is one example that comes to mind. Faced with the decision to run the restaurant or get my stepfather out of jail, my mother simply used poor judgment. The effect on me was the same. Eleven years old, left alone to run a restaurant, and trying to cook breakfast for people when I had never cooked it for myself wasn't a good memory to store away.

Sometimes our telling of the stories is slanted because it is about us—we are the participants in the events and cannot maintain a neutral position. For this reason, we tell it our way or the way we want others to hear it. Yet, the problem gets complicated because we come to believe it the way we tell it. I think this is one of the reasons people complain. They want to compel us to feel the world the way they feel it rather than investing their energy into changing the situation.

This has led to another thought. It seems to me that our stories sometimes indicate where we are stuck emotionally, mentally and/or spiritually. Something happened that was negative or painful. We are part of the event. We experience it, feel it and live it. It all gets meshed together. For years, when someone would say, "Tell me about yourself." What I would tell was like pushing the button on a tape recorder.

This is what I would play: "I was born in Alabama. My dad died when I was 9. My mother married again to a man who struggled with alcohol. We moved a lot." That story was the defining one for me. Over and over I repeated it word for word and emotion for emotion.

I didn't realize until much later that I was stuck. Emotionally I had not processed and unpackaged all of those events. I was still grieving, still feeling the emotional pain. I still hurt like I was a 9-year-old little boy. I don't think this is unusual or odd but rather common and reinforces my point. As we retell the story, we are reliving the loss, grief and pain, but we are stuck. We haven't processed or healed from the experience. The feelings are still with us and very much alive. Anchored to the past, the emotional energy is trapped in an event that took place 1, 5, 10 or 30 years ago.

This is one of the ways we share a strong connection to the people around us. Everyone has a story. Amanda Fogarty Hall used these words to describe her experience:

> Everyone has a story, but so many of them have the same thread. When it seems like you are the only one with a story like yours, it is nice to hear that there are other people out there just like you—even if it makes you sad for them at the same time. My story has helped me grow and become stronger in my love and in my walk with God. My story has made me grow mentally and emotionally by enabling me to help my children learn they are more important to me than anything else in the world. This is very different than my childhood. There are parts of my story that still hurt me when I think about it, but I do not want to change my past in any way, because the past is what makes me the person I am today.

Now, I think that our stories are our path to healing and wholeness. With time, I have come to look back at my journey, see the people, relive the events and realize no one really intended to do me harm. I don't think my mother woke up one day and decided to leave me alone as punishment. She was married to an alcoholic who could not hold down a regular job, and she had to make a living. She was the only one who could do it. So her frequently leaving me alone wasn't an emotional or hateful decision. Out of all the struggles and responsibilities she faced, I was one of the least challenging ones. I could make it on my own, and I did.

As we retell our experiences, we get to review, slow down, unpack the baggage and look for layers of meaning that we can now understand with a little more insight and a lot less emotion. We may also find that things didn't happen as we imagined. There may have been other influences or factors beyond our control. Also, we may see that people did not operate with the motives or purposes we have assumed and assigned to them for so long.

Writing a New One

Finally, here is the most powerful insight I have discovered about our stories of life. I believe that when healing of the past takes place, we can begin to see ways to write another version. With some situations and losses, we may not want to do so. Yet, if we don't, we may miss the most important opportunity of all—to transform the pain of life into a useful purpose. Instead of being held hostage to an event in the past, we can make small steps toward making life more meaningful for ourselves and those around us.

We have the power to pick up the pen, select a clean sheet of paper and write a different narrative. It isn't necessarily the one we thought we would be living, but it is ours. It is the one we create from the pieces of the puzzle we have in front of us. Suddenly life isn't taking place by accident or in a random manner. Rather we make choices about the future and what takes place in an intentional way.

To me, this is one of the goals of this book. How can we take the NOs that life has brought our way and begin to write a YES that we can embrace? Ultimately, it is the question of, "How can I recreate my life?" You can do it when you get tired of hearing the old story and you honestly desire to start writing a new one.

Powered by Beliefs

An Active Delivery System

Words form the foundation of our lives. At a very early age, we learn the basic ones of *momma, daddy, dog, cat* and *ball.* When these are in place, we move on to the more important ones of *play, love, hugs* and *hold you.* With these building blocks, a child begins to describe the events in their lives. These become their stories, and before long, stories become memories of good times or maybe not-so-good times. Beliefs are formed based upon the stories. We begin to develop an idea of how well we can function in certain settings based upon the way we look at ourselves and our ability to accomplish something.

To me, our memory works like a complex package delivery system. We create memories, we store memories, and we retrieve memories. This ongoing process is internal for each person and influenced by their choices in life. This automated process becomes our way of making sense of what takes place in our world and relationships.

Carol Mathias states that, "Our memory around a YES or NO experience creates a neurological superhighway; memory thoughts that fire together wire together. That is why change is so difficult. That becomes the mental filing cabinet."

I call my place *Memory Lane.* For others, their memory becomes this larger internal storage facility for all of their stories and words. Like file folders in a big cabinet, there are tabs to help locate events, times or special moments. A few are neatly placed together in an organized manner. Others are thrown in there without any rhyme or reason, stacked one on top of the other. Our memory then becomes this resource for moments that are good or not so good.

A friend Brenda Oglesby describes it this way:

> *Memories help me relive precious moments of loved ones who have passed away, of funny times, of tears shared and of an overwhelming feeling of being totally loved. I do have sad memories also: memories of missed opportunities to spend time with family, memories of harsh and unnecessary words spoken, memories of things I wish I could go back and grasp with eagerness instead of dread. Because in hindsight I know I would do it better. Memories help remind me there are no do-overs in life. You have to try and get it right the first time.*

There isn't anything wrong with this process. On occasion, we might want to erase our memories. We find that there is too much hurt or disappointment attached to the ones we have stored away.

Throwing Life Away

Several years ago I read a column in our local paper, "The Citizen and Georgian," written by Violet Moore. She described a Sunday afternoon walk with friends on a piece of land out in the country. As they strolled over the property, they came upon a large ditch and found a suitcase that had been thrown into it. They opened up the suitcase to find hundreds and hundreds of family pictures. Her words were, "It seemed like someone was trying to throw away all of their memories."

We may feel a desire to get rid of old memories. April Hair Cross felt the same way. Her words serve as a healthy reminder that in the pain there is also value.

For years, I tried my best to forget both the good and bad times from my first marriage. There were too many bad memories that were so painful that I wished the 7 ½ years we were together could have been erased from my memory. Then I remembered the friendships that developed from this marriage, and in a roundabout way that period of time led me to meet my current husband, whom I have loved now for 14 years. If I had been granted my wish, I would not be where I am now—married with two boys. My former mother-in-law recently passed away, and I had the opportunity to go to her funeral. I faced my past and realized that I missed my former in-laws. No matter how much you want to forget, maybe, just maybe, it is actually better to remember.

A good memory can help us hold onto the moments in life when our lives changed forever. These are times of celebration and happiness. Jill Elliott shared a day when her life reached a fork in the road.

That day the adoption agency called at 5:36 p.m. to tell my husband and me that we had a beautiful 7 lb., 7 oz. baby girl, and we could pick her up. Because this process had not worked out on an earlier occasion, we had delayed getting anything ready for a nursery. Therefore, all I had was one tube of Desitin ointment. In 1984, there were no 24-hour stores. There was one drugstore open all night near where we lived in Atlanta. We went there to buy tiny diapers and bath soap. That was it. We picked our baby girl up at 9:39 the next morning, and I took her to my office first. By 3:30 p.m. that same afternoon, it looked like I'd had four baby showers—there were presents galore for her. She seemed to belong to everyone, and so many of our friends treated her like she was one of their own. It was a delicious time. She's now 26, and my life changed forever.

The event Jill shares is one that touches all of us. The expected call came at an unpredictable time. Being unprepared for the big moment, there isn't much you can do about it. Yet, there is so much joy to be shared, and it strikes me that everything she needed was provided.

A good memory can be a curse. You can remember the time you didn't act with kindness or understanding. You remember when you should have said the unspoken message but didn't do it. Over time this memory creation process begins to shape our beliefs. A story becomes a memory that becomes a belief about yourself or about life.

A Belief Forms

One year my family moved to a city in Mississippi where I attended the seventh grade. I was in a physical education class where we were playing basketball. As a part of the practice, scrimmage games were set up between different classes. The basketball coach put me into the game, but I wasn't playing very well. He called a timeout and pulled me out of the game. When I came to the sidelines, he asked, "What in the world are you doing out there?" At that point in time, I didn't have a clue. From this brief episode, a belief was formed. It was unspoken and quietly stored away. It was the question, "What in the world are you doing?" This game of basketball ended some 47 years ago, but today the question still lingers when I face an uncomfortable situation or challenge. A little voice raises the question again, "What in the world are you doing?"

Beliefs become four-lane highways of information between our memories and our current life experience. As we face a new situation, we send a message to our memory storage system to retrieve an experience related to this event. The memory shoots into our thought process and along with it either an empowering or limiting belief that will lead us to take action accordingly.

If we have heard NO words and had many NO stories, it becomes more difficult to recover from adversity. Why? You get tired and weary of making the effort. Your memory recovery system retrieves all of the mistakes, hurts and pain as a reminder of how difficult the process is going to be. If we have heard YES words along the way and combined those with YES stories, we have the foundation for making a rebound after adversity strikes. Why? Because we have already experienced the movement of life in a positive direction, there is momentum for doing it again. Like exercise there is stretch-ability and adaptability already in place.

Is this how the process really works? I don't know. This is how I see it working. This is also how I learned to move beyond the NOs that had built up over the years. I had to take an intentional walk down Memory Lane. I stopped at each memory, took out all of the big boxes, and some of the small packages as well. Then I began to unpack those that had some energy still in them and examine the way I had stored them away initially. From this I was able to move from looking at my life as a series of negative events to one that was spiced with enough adversity to help me realize that we walk on the same road, and we are all looking for solutions on how to deal with the pain. In this search, I discovered a sense of meaning and purpose. There was peace. I found a way for my internal and external worlds to work together. I found an alignment in life that brought a sense of contentment and purpose. I think we all desire to find wholeness where all of the memories, beliefs and broken places come together to form a consistent whole. We want to feel good about our lives.

Waiting on Coming Attractions

In a Theater Near You

Whenever you go to the movies, you can expect to see a number of trailers or previews for coming attractions. Special scenes are included to create a "teaser" or desire for the audience to see the next blockbuster hit when it is released, usually in just a few weeks or months.

I have often thought our expectations for life play out in a similar way. We focus on every movement a Hollywood star makes. We observe the lives of the rich and famous. Marketing messages bombard us with what we need, want, and must have to be happy in life. Through television we see thin, athletic people and believe we should be the same. Before long, an image begins to form of what life will be like for us. It will include our hopes and desires for health, family life, children, well-being, financial stability, success and many more wishes for the future.

These thoughts and expectations become the fuel for our dreams in life. It becomes a script that we recite to ourselves at every stage. I will grow up, get an education, go to work, make lots of money, find someone who loves me, get married, stay married forever, have beautiful and healthy children, live in a wonderful home, be removed from harm or adversity, and live happily ever after. For some, this is called *the American Dream*. One day we will achieve all that our heart desires. We will be healthy. We will climb the ladder of success. We will have happy families with loving mothers and fathers, obedient children, and stress-free living. Furthermore, we are entitled to happiness. We live in America.

I have exaggerated this a little for the sake of illustration. It seems that in every relationship and experience, we bring a preconceived view of how things should go. These are our expectations for life, love, relationships and all facets of our existence.

Living My Movie

I thought my life would begin and end in Hamilton, Ala. I saw myself going to school, graduating and working in that small town. I believed I would end up being a teacher or farmer one day. I would live along Highway 278. A day in July changed all of my plans. My father died. A year or so later my mother married a man from Georgia, and my life script was suddenly rewritten. I didn't have a lot of input. My expectations pointed me in one direction while events took me in another one. Isn't that the way it goes for most of us? I think that it is.

I have watched this occur in many different settings. A young lady begins the process of planning her wedding, and immediately you hear what she wants to take place as far as location, time, people, arrangements and details. She marries the man of her dreams. Their life together begins. Along the way life happens. His work requires a move to another state. They have a baby. An affair takes place. They fall out of love. Suddenly, the coming attraction that was supposed to take place doesn't. It ends in divorce. Two wonderful people now feel the loss and end of a once promising relationship. They go their separate ways with all of the pain from shattered dreams.

I hear it when I work with teams in the work place. I will ask, "What do you expect out of the other members of your team?"

The responses will be similar: "I expect fairness, communication, understanding and patience." Without variation, the response is the same. Yet, here are dedicated professionals who desire the same outcome locked into immobilizing conflict. Egos get in the way. One person's need for privacy competes with another person's need to discuss intimate details of their life in a public setting. As a result, mature and educated people get stuck. Relationships suffer. Communication stops. Performance takes a hit. This isn't what they expected when they initially chose to work with this particular employer.

Or, I see it with careers. A person completes their education, sends in a resume and finds a position. Soon you can hear their thoughts on how life is going to go according to their plans. Based upon income, they purchase a home and car. They expand their financial commitments. Then one day the economy takes a downturn. The company or organization makes changes. Suddenly, positions are being eliminated, responsibilities are re-assigned, and pressure becomes more intense. Broken expectations fall to the floor like a shattered glass.

There are a variety of ways that we practice expectations. When I was younger I really thought that I would be famous. I don't mean that in an egotistical kind of way. Rather, it was a quiet thought that was ever present. I don't think I am the only one who has held this belief. Stephen Jones writes, "I expected to change the world—to make it a better place. Now, I think less globally. I just want to do the best for my children—my little corner of this big world."

We expect marriages to be based on love and last forever. April Hair Cross shares, "As a child of divorce, I knew the odds were not in my favor. I hoped and prayed that my marriage would survive. But the marriage was not the best in the world—it was mentally and physically abusive. He left, and I was devastated thinking that was the best I could do and I would never find anyone else. Along came my current husband who, as of yesterday, I have been married to for 15 years."

Push the Play Button Now

I asked some of my friends what they expected out of life. Here are some of the responses I received:

Nancy Conley Smith: I expected to go to college, have a fulfilling career, get married, stay married, have children...the usual. I have learned that God often has different plans/expectations for me. While this has been frustrating at times (like being unable to get pregnant immediately when we wanted children, getting divorced, etc.), I have come to realize that God knows more than I do, and the timing of reaching the milestones in my life has a purpose and is often a much better plan than the one I had, even if I didn't realize it at the time!

I also think our attitude and outlook on life has an impact on our expectations. I have seen people with difficult personal circumstances have wonderful attitudes about life and be able to uplift everyone around them. On the other hand, there are people that seem to have everything going for them, but they display attitudes that make no one want to be near them. I am not sure how attitude plays into our expectations, but I do strongly feel there is a link. I think people with good attitudes make the most of their life expectations and deal with the disappointments in a positive way when their expectations do not live up to reality.

Amanda Fogarty Hall: "I thought I was going to get married during college to my high school boyfriend,

become a teacher and have two children—a boy and a
girl. Well, life did not work out that way, but God has been
way better to me than I even deserved, and I would not
trade my life and my five babies for anything in this
world."

Judi Payton: *"Children in our family were raised in
almost a fairytale world, it seems. We were not rich in
material goods, but we were millionaires when it came to
love. I thought that everyone could be trusted; that if we
respect people they will respect us; that people would not
betray us. I expected to marry, raise a family, and be
secure in a nice, neat life with someone who loved me. By
now I should be retiring and enjoying life. Needless to say,
things did not turn out so nice and neat. But there is one
thing I do know— God has never abandoned me. He gave
me children and grandchildren to love, and they are
always there for me. He always sees me through whatever
hardships and heartaches come my way, and I know he
has much better plans for me than I have ever had before.
The best is yet to be."*

Angee Knight McKee: *"I guess I thought everything
would go according to my plan. Unfortunately when
things didn't, I often dug in my heels and tried to stay
with the plan, even though it obviously wasn't working
for me. Now don't get me wrong—a lot of things did work
out well for me. But in hindsight, my best life happened
when I was willing to move in a new direction and tell
fear to take a back seat!"*

Tiffany Lowe-Jones: *"Growing up, the greatest expectation I had was to just "Be Happy!" I'm sure most people can relate in some way to this. However, as simple as that may seem, we can make this quite a complex and strategic plan by putting far too much emphasis on the idea of "ending up" happy rather than just "being" happy. As I grow spiritually each day, I have learned to just "be"—roll with whatever happens. Instead of trying to control every angle of life by focusing on expectations and ideas of the perfect life, we can reap much greater rewards if we can just "be" in the moment!"*

These stories share a similar theme. You can hear a loud and clear, "I expected events to go a certain way." When we step back from our lives for a few moments and look with as much objectivity as we can muster at ourselves, a truth begins to emerge: We *believe* life should go our way. It seems we think we are in control of all events that take place and almost seem offended when something comes along that makes us change plans. Yet, we discover that in the adjustment comes a new discovery.

A Time to Rewind

When I began the process of writing, I knew words were important. They have been to me. I spent a lot of time trying to listen for the ones I longed to hear from good people who were busy trying to survive. With the words I found and the ones I couldn't find, I shaped stories about my life that I believed to be true. As a result I saw my life in comparison to others. I looked where I had done well, and I saw instances where I could never achieve the results I had hoped to realize. These beliefs influenced my expectations. It is amazing to me how much of our struggle takes place in our own hearts and minds. We listen and look for the YES we yearn to find, but then we discover NO. As a result, we accept NO as the final verdict, when in reality it is only the beginning point for discovery.

Before we move to a new section, let me ask you to take inventory. Look at the words you heard and the ones you wish you had heard. Walk back down Memory Lane. Listen to where there is celebration of the gift of your life. Notice where there are "haunted houses" that still bother you to this day. Look for the beliefs that have formed. Don't argue or disagree with them—notice what they are. Do these beliefs limit or empower you? Then play the tape. What are your expectations for yourself, for others and for the events you face? You may be surprised at what this walk through your life will reveal. I don't think there are any shortcuts to healing your life.

Sacred Stories

A Number of Years

I've dealt with healing both personally and as a therapist. I was a number of years truly healing from my brother's murder. The final time I dealt with it deeply was when I was on an Emmaus team. Saturday night after all the pilgrims left, I sat in the pew and began to cry from a place deeper in my soul than I ever imagined even existed. I was aware at the time that this was deep healing for me. As a therapist, I am constantly looking for the best way to help my clients get in touch with those deepest emotions. Our bodies, minds, emotions, and spirits are all connected and one affects another.

~*Carole Wren Nelson*

Not of this World

My YES is sometimes relative—no pun intended! This seems to especially be true in my work life—we will have patients come who are addicted to drugs, who don't have homes, who don't want their babies, etc. They have perfect deliveries and perfect babies and great luck. Then we have patients who are happy, healthy, well adjusted people in supportive marriages who experience infertility, difficult medical complications, and heartaches for no reason at all. Then there are the really sad cases when people have to bury their babies, or make very complicated decisions about what to do for their terminally ill *infants. Just when it seems like we can't see anything worse or we're about to break (as a staff of nurses) we'll have a wonderful patient with a heartwarming delivery (like the one we had once where a dad made it back from Afghanistan minutes before the baby was born). It will just barely keep us from going insane. It's like we get one good YES and it can cancel out all the junk. I think YES has more power than NO, because YES is not of this world and the NO comes from this world.*

    ~ Anonymous

I Reject Your Treatment of Me

I have thought a lot about your project and realize that it seems to me we all yearn for this YES and more often hear NO in our ordinary days. Just as a plant turns toward the sun, we turn toward the positive, the upbeat, the people who affirm who we are. And I agree I believe this is oh, so very important.

The drive to seek those things that uplift us is innate, I think. I was born in the 21st week and weighed in at 1 lb. 4 oz.—not much to look at and most definitely not the Gerber baby. Most of the affirmation I received growing up was from my paternal grandmother. She lived YES and she encouraged me to live YES. For most of my life my mother rejected me, first physically and then emotionally. She continues to reject me, and after 55 years of seeking her acceptance, this year I rejected her treatment of me and told her so. Now I could have a major pity party, but Grandmother even in Heaven would poo-poo this thought. I do not tell you this for any sympathy at all, only to emphatically state to live YES is to choose YES! And I sought to teach this to our children. I believe they in turn will someday teach their own. I know this concept echoes from them to their friends. I've seen it.

    ~Anonymous

The Runaway

I remember the last time I saw her at the house eating cereal like she hadn't eaten in days. I had seen her the week before when she was hiding out at a cheesy apartment a few miles down the road. She had looked lethargic and unkempt. I had convinced her to leave and return home, but she left again after only two nights at home. I knew something wasn't right. She wasn't herself and hadn't been the last two times I had seen her. I was scared. Something was very wrong. I could feel it.

I drove back to work with a knot in the pit in my stomach. What was my 19-year-old daughter doing? We had sent her off to college the year before, a happy and carefree almost-18-year-old. But she had been skipping classes and spending time with someone she had met on MySpace. I had spoken to him several times, and each time he had a pipe dream of becoming a physical therapist or getting a high-paying job or going to college, but WHAT was he doing in the meantime? And what had he done for his 27 years? Things weren't adding up. I knew he was not good for our daughter, but she was not hearing my husband and me when we urged her to go to class.

I soon learned she was driving west. First she spent a couple of weeks in Colorado, and then she kept traveling until she reached "Cali" (as she called it). Fortunately for me, three angels kept me informed of her whereabouts and needs. Three of her best friends called me when they spoke to her. They let me know that she was safe and on her journey.

Now comes the difficult part. My eyes are tearing and my stomach is turning just thinking of the feelings I had. I prayed and cried myself to sleep every night. I woke up in the middle of the night just to cry myself to sleep again and again. I cried when I thought of her and when others asked about her. We were on so many prayer chains that I lost count. I prayed that God would keep her safe that day and help her make better decisions so she would want to get out of her situation. I prayed for her not to go

84

hungry, and I prayed for her health. I could not relax. I could not be content until my baby was home. I knew others were right when they constantly reminded me we had raised her right, God was with her, and she would eventually return. I just didn't know when, and not knowing was overwhelming, even debilitating.

She drove our car across the country, and so that we would not be enabling her to continue this lifestyle, my husband flew to California and worked with the police to regain our car without her knowledge. We were informed by our insurance company that we would be liable if they were driving and anything happened to anyone or anything else, so we retrieved the car and had it transported back to the east coast. She was very angry with us when she discovered we had taken her "wheels." She was sure that she would not be able to find a job or get to it without transportation and it was, of course, our fault. It was tough love.

Tough on my husband and me, that is. We were certain if we could ever get her away from him, we could have talked to her and convinced her he was not a good influence on her, and she would come home. Finally, her biological father suggested she come visit him in Kansas. She agreed and went to his house for the week. He tried to make communication with the guy difficult, but they found a way, and after only a few days, her father came home from work and discovered again she was gone. We couldn't figure out how she got the airfare or where they were getting money. Of course we could only think the worst. How does someone who doesn't work obtain money?

I would occasionally get a call from her telling me she had nothing to eat or that she had been to a shelter to eat a meal. It breaks my heart, even now, four years later, as I sit here and recall that horrific experience. My son, a very impressionable 10-year-old at the time looked at me one day and said, "Mom, it's kind of embarrassing having a sister like her." He knew it was difficult and unlike anything we had ever experienced. I felt guilt and shame that he had to be part of all of that. It was way too heavy for him. I worried she would not be able to eat, so I sent

85

her grocery gift cards. I was concerned that they might be using drugs and did not want to contribute to harming them or enable them to continue living in that manner, so I thought gift cards were safer than cash. I also sent her some clothes and some sheets when she confessed she didn't have a jacket and was cold at night. I just wanted to keep the communication open.

One day, she called, and I told her a friend of hers was getting married, and she was invited. She reminded me (like I didn't remember) that she had no money. I volunteered to buy her ticket but said that I would prefer it to be one-way. She, of course, declined. I mustered up enough strength to offer to buy her a two-way ticket figuring it would be better to see her for a short while than not to see her at all. I want to say that everything I (and I mean WE—my wonderful husband was in this with me all the way) did was a road we had never traveled down before. Knowing what do to next was not easy. We were praying that God would lead her back to us. We didn't want to make decisions that would negatively impact that.

It was such a relief to see her. For the first time since she had left, we were elated. We were so happy to hug her, to kiss her, and to just lay eyes on her. She actually looked better than we expected. As I mentioned, your imagination can push you to think the worst. Anyway, we talked, heard about her situation, her new job as a barista, the car they had purchased, and the roommate they shared their new apartment with. We were careful not to judge, but just to be thankful we had that time together.

Before she boarded the plane to return to California, her friend shared a secret with me—she was pregnant. Part of me wanted to grab her and insist she stay with us, but

I knew that would not be helpful to the situation. I just kept the secret close to my heart and began a whole new set of prayers for the baby, my daughter and our entire family. I reminded her that we were here for her whenever she wanted to come home. I told her then—as I always have and always will—

that I love her. As we waved goodbye, tears were once again flowing.

Only about a week after she left, she called me on a Saturday morning and told me herself that she was expecting our grandchild. She said she was hungry and felt sick and just wanted a popsicle for the nausea. I put a few dollars on her debit card and instructed her to go to the grocery store and get some popsicles and something she could prepare for dinner.

Later that day, she called again and left us a message thanking us for the money and described the delicious dinner she had eaten. I listened to the message and smiled. For some reason (I am certain it was God speaking) I decided to try to call her back. We usually spoke only every other week or so. She wouldn't answer if I did call on most occasions, so I tried to be patient and wait for her to call us. Anyway, I called her and told her I had received her message and wanted to check to see how she was feeling.

Before I could even get it out, she was sobbing saying, "I want to come home. I want to come home." My husband immediately got on the phone, called a peace officer to their apartment and instructed her to slip into the bathroom and lock the door until the peace officer arrived. (I had never even heard of a PEACE officer before).

While he was talking to her on the phone, he found a flight out of their town at 6 the next morning (it was after 10 p.m. by that time) and scheduled a taxi to pick her up at 3:30 a.m. My heart was racing at full speed by this time. She had called us two times before begging to come home during her six months away, but the phone had been hung up before we could get the travel set up. He convinced her to stay both times before, and we knew it was still a possibility this time. In fact, we could hear him pleading with her to open the door and to talk to him. We prayed God would keep her on the phone with us as my husband worked his magic to get our baby back home. Eventually the officer arrived, asked "him" to leave for the night and told us on the *phone that he would ensure her safety. We did not sleep that night. We just prayed and cried, this time tears of hope and joy.*

Seeing her emerge from the dark walkway was like seeing an angel. We embraced and didn't want to let go. We just sat and held each other as we waited for the luggage to arrive. We soon found out where they were getting money....she had been able to get a $10,000 credit card and a car with a part-time job as a barista, and without a penny down. Unbelievable! ...as is this whole experience. Thank you so much, Dear Lord, for bringing her home to us safe and sound. Thank you for all she means to all of us today. And thank you for that beautiful little granddaughter that has brought us nothing but joy and happiness. She is truly a gift from above. Thank you so much for bringing our beautiful family together and for walking with us, protecting us and loving us each day.

~Carlene Jones Kelley

Giving Her the Right Words

When you ask our daughter, Lily Jane, a question, she usually nods her head yes. Now, this can be any question."Do you want milk? Do you want to go to bed? Do you want to go to school? Do you want to see Daddy?" and her answer is almost always YES and a big nod of the head. Sometimes her YES should be NO, like when I ask her if she wants a spanking, and she still says, "Yes!" What this tells me is that somewhere and at some point, Michael and I have done something right, because in her little world filled with NOs—"No, don't touch that!...No, don't put that in your mouth...No, you do not hit," she is hearing a lot of YES's. Hopefully this will carry through her entire life and teach her that in all of the NOs she will hear and probably say, that there should and will be many YES's.

~Laura Gregg Hardester

Instilled in Their Little Spirits

As a Speech and Language Pathology teacher, living YES can be a powerful tool in the lives of children with whom I work, and I have to remind myself of that on a daily basis. Academically, YES is not often an answer that comes easily to many of them. So in our classroom, we try to make sure it is instilled into their little spirits daily. Most of them struggle, especially in the area of reading and writing, and NO has been a constant theme for many of them. "No, that's not the word. No, that's not how you spell it. No, that's not the letter. No! Will you ever learn?"

Admittedly, it wasn't until after my first son was born and started school that I realized how much of an impact teachers can have on the self-esteem of students. It is these children that I feel equipped to help in some way. "Yes! I know reading is hard for you, but there is another way to learn, and we will teach you! Yes! You are so close—you are getting better and better each day! Yes! You did it—you can read!"

Then... there are those who also hear a resounding "No" at home, either directly or subtly. "No, you are not as good as your older brother. No, you don't ever listen. No, I don't love you unconditionally. No, you're not good enough for me...and you never will be."

So, how is my YES good enough for those? How can it measure up when others, significant others in their lives, are saying NO? Those are the ones with "YES" answers that come when I am sitting alone, and the house is quiet and still, and I picture their faces in my mind. My most powerful YES answers to them come as prayers, voiced not to them, but to the One who hears our prayers. "Yes! Let him be the one to break the cycle...of poverty, illiteracy, and addiction. Yes! Let her believe in herself when no one around her does...show her the way! Yes! Let them believe that love does exist, and it can be different one day." In the meantime, I can only hope that my YES can be heard clearly and calmly above the storm of NOs in their lives.

~*Lindsay Gregg Peaster*

Mema

The very first thing that came into my mind when I think about YES is my niece. She just turned 40, and she has held a special place in my heart since she was born. I was in college in Americus, Ga. and took off to Columbus as soon as I heard she was about to be born very prematurely. She was a seven-month baby and barely weighed 4 lbs. Yes, she did make it, and she became the baby sister that I never had.

My story began on Sunday, September 12, 2010. My niece, Dana, called to tell me that Mema, my mom and Dana's grandmother, was in the Emergency Room at a hospital in Columbus, Ga. She was 87 at the time and not in good health. So, you can see my real story also starts off as "Oh, NO!... Oh no, she was diagnosed with congestive heart failure! Oh, no, they didn't have a room available for her until the next afternoon. Oh, no, a private room wasn't available. Oh, no, she had two different roommates in two days."

Yes, the roommates added some kind of stress relief for one reason or another. Yes, on Wednesday we were finally moved into a private room even though we thought she would be released that day. Yes, to a really nice room that seemed like a very nice motel room, but, No when we found out she was not going to be released.

A big YES goes to all the nurses, doctors, staff, and techs who provided excellent care and service to Mema while she was there. They all need to be presented the Health Care Employee of the Month Award at the hospital. Yes, to every one of them because we learned valuable information from each one of them—things that would not only help Mema's health, but her family's. Yes, to all my friends and family who called, texted or even visited. Yes, to you, Randy Gregg, who—though you were not Mema's preacher, she considered you to be—took the time to come and visit. She said for many years that she wanted you to do her funeral.

Yes, to my friends who visited or called every day. You know who you are. Yes, because you care enough about her that you call her by her own special name, Mema, too. Yes, to Jackson, my husband, who always offered support and understanding. Yes, to my children, Michael and Lauren, who were in constant touch with us during the week. Yes, to four of her little great-grand children who showed their love by either asking lots of questions or visiting.

The great big YES goes to my niece Dana, her husband, Troy, and her two sons, Chase and Cason. This very special granddaughter opened up her home almost four years ago to Mema when it was decided she couldn't live alone anymore. Dana had always told Troy that she was a package deal. She meant that one day Mema would come and live with them because of the special love that only a grandmother and granddaughter can have for each other. Yes, to that special love that is truly amazing.

Yes, to after seven days Mema was released with many strict orders to follow diet-wise. Yes, to the doctor who cared enough about her to keep her long enough to diagnose all of her problems. Yes, to "Mrs. Dash," because Mema sure can't have salt in her food anymore. Yes, to me being recently retired from teaching and able to stay with her every day and night so that she wouldn't be alone. Yes, to my niece being there with us most of the time except when she had to see about her two little boys and husband.

Mema had to return to the hospital many times after that week long stay. She went back in December of that same year and stayed over a month. I had a YES story during that long stay. I was able to spend Christmas Eve night with her and wake up with her on Christmas morning so that Dana could be with her two little boys. We decorated her room to look like Christmas and read Christmas stories. My daughter, Lauren, and her boyfriend had become engaged right before Christmas. They came and surprised her Christmas morning to announce their engagement. Mema said that she had known it because Matthew had told her during the summer that he was asking Lauren to marry him at Christmas time. She said she kept a good secret. We all had a good laugh, and that was definitely a YES.

Mema was placed under Hospice care during that stay in the hospital. It was a sad decision but we also did it with the understanding that she could get better. My son, Michael, and grandson, Emory, were there when we all made the move to Hospice. It was nice to have Dana, Troy, Chase, Cason, Michael, Emory, and myself there to make the transition easier.

Mema was able to come home, but she never really regained her strength and was never able to walk again. Dana and Hospice took wonderful care of her, and I came to help a lot.

Four of Mema's great-grandchildren became very close to her during her stay with Dana. I will always be thankful for the closeness that Chase and Cason and my two little grandchildren, Emory and Ella Claire, developed with her.

Mema celebrated her 88th birthday on July 17, 2011. We had a big party for her at Dana's house. She got to see many friends and family that day. We all knew the end was coming very soon, but none of us wanted to accept it, especially Mema. Dana, Troy, Chase, Cason, Emory, Ella Claire, and I all had a good visit with her the week of July 25th. We played games on the floor beside her bed, and she even fussed at us when we got too loud. It was a very special time.

My grandchildren and I had to leave to go back and get ready to start school. I received that very sad call from Dana on July 30th that Mema was dying. I could hear Dana asking Mema if she wanted to go to Hospice or stay here and she said, "Here!" That was the last word I heard her say. She died shortly after that with her precious granddaughter Dana by her side. It was as it should have been. NO, to the fact that we lost Mema that day, but so many YES's through the years for her deep, deep love for her family and friends.

I am not able to make any more Mema Stories, but I cherish the ones that I have. She was a wonderful, talented, smart, feisty, sweet, loyal, caring and loving person. Yes, to her life and to the people whose lives she touched along the way.
~Charlene Wright Jackson

Reflections

Where do you go for emotional and spiritual nourishment? What feeds your spirit? Who feeds your soul? What are your sources for life? Are these reliable and worthy of who you are as a person?

If we are honest, we will admit that we have a "memory bank" of words and stories stockpiled in the closets of our spirit—filed away, labeled and ready for retrieval. These are easily accessed by mentioning a few "code words." The statement, "Do you remember the time the lightning struck?" automatically takes you to a time, place and event.

Unfortunately, most of our words, stories, memories, beliefs and expectations lie hidden below the surface of our lives. Yielding major influence in every action, decision, relationship and conversation, no one ever sees them or knows that they exist. Only when we share a memory do we toss out hints about what lies underneath the layers of who we are.

To grow toward the future, takes courage—more than we have sometimes. It takes honesty and a desire to grow to be able to pull out all of the file folders, look at the labels, and discover the ultimate truth of what pushes, guides and even controls our keyboard of life.

Entrances and Exits

Prayer for Entrances and Exits

Heavenly Father,

We come to you as the creator of life and relationships. You have placed within us a desire to share companionship and journey with others. With gratitude, we thank you for the many people whom we have met, loved and lost. This gaining and losing of relationships has allowed us to experience the full range of loss and joy. We are richer. We are wiser. We are forever changed.

Guide us now to hear our YES and NO for life that we may live intentionally each day. May we look beyond imaginary doors and labels to see the deeper movement of your spirit holding us close through the transitional moments of endings and new beginnings.

In Christ's Name,

Amen

Signs on the Door

I have a favorite coffee shop on the corner of a busy street where I like to sit and watch the world. It offers soft music, gentle conversation and wonderful latte`s. It is a place for observing a small town and what happens as the day wakes up for a new beginning. With a soft rumble of noise, traffic moves by like a line of ants on the way to a picnic. It is easy to watch the routine of everyday life unfold. The regular crowd shows up on schedule to drink coffee, eat breakfast and connect with one another. The mail carrier stops by at the same time to deliver envelopes and parcels. Delivery trucks show up with packages to be opened.

There is one facet of this coming and going of people that particularly intrigues me—the signs on the doors of the coffee shop. They are quite simple; enter and exit. It can be a source of a great deal of action. The doors are clearly marked, and it is amusing to watch people try to push when the sign clearly reads *pull.* So, they press forward with the weight of their body only to bump into the clear glass of the door. Then there is the immediate effort at recovery. How do you look cool when you have just plastered your face against an immoveable object? Or, how do you regain your composure when you just banged a door that is clearly marked? I shouldn't be surprised. I often don't get life's signs right myself. I miss the signals. I fail to notice the turns and twists. I don't navigate all of the turns well, and I slam into immoveable objects.

People, events, and experiences are constantly entering or exiting our lives. Some occur with our permission, while others leave unexpectedly without any announcement at all. This coming and going creates unexpected adjustments.

For many years, I interpreted the events from my early life as negative ones. I could see where people had wandered off physically and emotionally. Over time, I sanded the story down to the point that I could illustrate the NO of life with great detail. The problem with this approach is that it kept me stuck. I would look at the characters as the source of all of my problems. While my description might have been accurate, the results were devastating. I stayed a victim. "Poor Randy" became a little boy who lost his father, and his mother remarried an alcoholic who couldn't hold a job or take responsibility for his life. I now wonder if it is the events we experience or how we process those events emotionally or mentally that creates the most lasting impact.

There were two words present all of the time, though I did not see them until I was much older. They are two of the most basic: YES and NO. I write them with capital letters for a reason; not to communicate shouting or speaking with a loud voice, but rather to express the sense that these are two of life's great sources of energy.

YES opens doors, creates opportunities, affirms purpose, agrees with intent, and suggests that events will move in a desired direction.

NO closes doors, limits opportunities, negates purpose, disagrees with intent, and fails to see events moving in a desired direction.

These words, like all others, are introduced and defined for us by other people. In many ways, children are shaped by the words, memories, beliefs and expectations of those around them. These values become their "Inherited YES." It is the one given, borrowed, or inherited from those who love them. YES becomes the door for all of the good, positive opportunities that can take place in the child's life.

NO becomes the door that limits, protects or sets boundaries.

In an ideal world, those who love us would use these words as effective tools for shaping and nurturing the life of the child, so that the good and positive would grow while the negative or limited would serve to protect. Unfortunately we don't live in an ideal world. We live in a real one where adults don't always see the need to nurture. They don't define the words well. They don't set clear boundaries. They don't create positive memories. They aren't there to protect.

Some families do a wonderful job of emotional development and support. They are committed, present and involved in the life of the child. They set a great example for the child to develop a healthy mind, body and spirit. It is a calling to be fulfilled more than a task to be completed.

Healthy families recognize the power of the gatekeepers and assign them clear responsibilities. YES becomes a driving force for realizing potential and growing into a person of worth and value. NO becomes the boundary word that protects and sets limits so the person can live with some sense of protection and safety.

These are good words. They hold much influence in our lives. They become our source of power when we realize we can develop our own gatekeepers and assign them the responsibility of serving our needs to live a healthy life.

The reasons I believe these two words are so important go back to the entrance and exit. Some people, events and experiences enter our lives without permission. Some leave without permission as well. Out of the confusing shuffle of moments, we create who we are. I hope we can all learn to live YES to life, faith, hope, love, hurt, setback and celebration. It is a big life and we need these words to give us direction.

On A Crowded Road

I have always enjoyed the comic strip, "Frank and Ernest," created by Bob Thaves.[vii] One segment in particular captured a thought I have long remembered. There are three slides. In the first one, Frank and Ernest are looking at a tall ladder with a sign posted nearby that reads "Ladder of Success." In the second image, there is the same scene but the two guys are looking up the ladder toward the sky. In the third one, Frank says, "I was hoping to find an escalator."

Many of us are like Frank. We want our path to success to work automatically so we can step on it and be immediately transported to our destination of happiness. We are not alone in that wish. In fact, we hold more than one belief about how things should work. These are stored away as expectations.

While expectations are mostly unspoken, they are a powerful force that influences everything we do. I often wonder if perhaps we think life should be more like what Garrison Keillor describes in Lake Wobegon when he closes out a radio broadcast from this fictional town. He states, "And that is how it is in Lake Wobegon, where all the women are strong, all the men are good looking, and all the children are above average."[viii]

Simple Thoughts

Basically, expectations are simple thoughts that we hold about how the world should operate. *Should* is the operative word in the statement. These ideas come to us from a variety of sources. Certainly, they come to us from family. Who hasn't heard their mother or father say, "Now, good girls or boys do the right thing."

An expectation is instantly born. You now expect all good people to behave in a certain manner. This thought packs a bag and travels with us as we start a family, raise children, and experience stress—as we soon learn, many good people don't do the right thing.

I invited some friends to offer their thoughts on expectations. I soon learned there is a wide range of possibilities. Listen to the silent influences each statement below offers and consider how a single thought like one of these can impact your life in a big way.

- *I will be accepted and valued.* Stacye Whitt Clark
- *I will not be a disappointment or an embarrassment to my family.* Myra Junkins Cameron
- *Early in life, we believe we will make a difference. Later in life, we hope that we have.* Lisa Palmer Talley
- *We will live longer than our children.* Linda Edwards
- *My family will be close.* Dianne Gregg
- *I will get what I want.* Tiffany Lowe- Jones
- *If we choose to do the "right" thing, people will agree with and support us.* Angee Knight McKee

If you read each statement above carefully, you can begin to hear themes emerge. These are centered on our well-being, family, work and personal achievement. In some ways, we all want the same things out of life. We all walk on a very busy highway headed to our definition of happiness.

Each person shared basic thoughts. To me, it is like letting the Energizer Bunny take over your thought process.[ix] These quiet ideas can "keep on going" as they energize relationships, events and conversations. The energy can be positive or negative.

The Movie Begins

One Saturday in the fall, my wife, Dianne, and I were invited to a party. It was on a Saturday night when the University of Georgia was playing a football game. Instead of sitting around the den watching the game on television, we set up an LCD projector and a large screen out in the yard. Being outside allowed everyone to sit in lawn chairs, eat barbeque and visit with friends. It was a lot of fun. The evening had the feel of a real tail-gate party.

I sometimes wonder if our thought process works in a similar way. In every conscious moment there is a projector running that creates this living movie playing in our minds. The images being displayed are our expectations of life. This active cinema reveals what we think "should be happening" in this moment, in an event, in this relationship or in this conversation.

It becomes very interesting when we realize that we are the only one who has access to the movie being played. So, we talk to our children, and the images on our screen might be "children do their home work in a timely manner." In our conversation, our child might say, "I don't like the teacher, I want to play, and I am not going to do the homework now." A lengthy and heated conversation would then flow out of the conflict between these two world views.

Suppose your expectation is that "bad things don't happen to good people." Suddenly, a friend is injured in a wreck. You go to visit and to comfort her. It will be difficult to offer any encouragement when your movie of how life should operate conflicts with the reality of the one you see in front of you.

Or, imagine that you hold onto the idea that people get married and you make the marriage work at all costs. That is a wonderful ideal, but it may be tested when one spouse becomes abusive or mistreats the other partner. What do you do—stay in the relationship no matter what, or get out of the relationship and violate one of your basic truths about marriage?

Expectations and Stress

In some ways, expectations offer support. There is the hope or desire that plans will go a certain way. This anticipation brings energy to all that we do. This inner power sits waiting to be utilized. However, expectations can create problems. Since they are silent and unknown, these guiding forces of life often operate like a stealth fighter jet. They fly under the radar. They are the hidden guests present in every moment of our life.

In addition, some become unrealistic. As Brandy Nelson Elrod mentioned, "I expect life will be fair." This guiding principle will create a lot of frustration and hurt. Why? Because life isn't fair. We know that a tornado operates independent of human influence, a hurricane changes course at will, and an earthquake can strike at any time.

When these become personalized, the potential for damage grows. If I hold the belief that "I should be available to friends or family 24/7," I have just set myself up for a lot of heartache. Anytime someone needs me, I feel the need to be there. Anytime the phone rings, I must answer. Anytime there is a request, I will strive to fulfill it. If I am not careful, I can spend all of my time pleasing others and never meet my own needs.

A Timely Question

With time and age, we may discover that some of our expectations about life are not true or they have become outdated. When I was young, I expected to run like the wind. As I have aged, I may do well to walk at a brisk pace. When younger, we may have dreamed of becoming the ruler of the universe. As we age, we hope we can touch one other person in a positive way.

Maybe we learned expectations from our family. We may have absorbed them from our culture. Or, we may have developed them in response to a life event. Whatever the source, the impact is the same. They can create stress.

There comes a time to put our unspoken beliefs to the test. It is healthy to question the authenticity, value and truth in each one. This takes courage, but it is worth the effort. I cannot offer a complete strategy for addressing unrealistic expectations. I do offer one simple step: question your beliefs. Why do you believe that you will meet "Prince Charming" and live "happily ever after?" When did that thought begin? Did it come from a movie, a book or your Aunt Matilda?

This one step moves your life from unconscious to conscious living. Rather than cruise on automatic pilot, you question beliefs that you assumed to be true and begin to test them against the reality of life. There will be some adjustment. There may be pain. It is difficult to realize that our beliefs, fantasies or expectations may not be valid any longer. I remember the first time I watched the "Wizard of Oz." It was a magical moment. Then I realized the wizard wasn't a wizard at all...there really isn't a magical person behind the curtain. Instead, we surrender control of our lives to unseen beliefs acquired over time that may not be reliable any longer.

Unfortunately, many live out their days without ever asking, "Why do I hold this expectation?" and allow untested beliefs to pull the lever behind the curtain of their life.

Enter YES

Somewhere in my early years, I bought into the idea that all of my world would be YES. Maybe it was my age and innocence. I didn't think life would be without problems or concerns, but I didn't believe that the people I loved would ever become sick and die, imagine a time when I would struggle with loss and grief, or anticipate the dark clouds of doubt and uncertainty. I could only visualize the possibilities and opportunities. Everything would go the way I wanted, or at least I hoped it would.

At the time, I didn't realize that this innate optimism becomes a driving force for us. When we speak and live YES, we tap into a powerful source of energy. It means we believe that doors will open. We look at events and people in a positive light. We search for options. We trust there will be solutions to all of our dilemmas.

In recent months, I have given additional thought to the word, *Y...E...S*, and realize it influences us in more ways than I initially imagined. YES becomes the affirmation or approval I desire to hear; acceptance I express to the events, ideas, and people around me; permission I give to myself or others; agreement I make; and surrender to a particular idea or course of action. In essence, it becomes my energy for being alive and present in my life. All of these influences shape my YES and your YES to be who we are.

When we practice and live it long enough, I believe YES becomes the emotional, mental and spiritual language we speak, to ourselves and others, in response to the events and people we encounter. To me, it is more than just being optimistic or having a positive attitude. It is the ability to face the adversity; accept the reality and pain; deal with the issues so that healing takes place; and recreate your inner world to continue living in spite of the setbacks, loss, hurt and doubt. There are those who see the good, beautiful and lovely in all situations. They have learned to speak the language of YES. This way of looking, interpreting and talking did not come easily. Deep within they have discovered that there is an energy available to them that goes beyond expectation or explanation. Their answer to the challenges isn't to *give up* or *give in* but rather to *go on* with the faith and hope they have embraced internally, rather than be stopped by any external reality.

It touches us at the deepest level of our experience. This affects the way we explain events to ourselves. It shapes the way we respond to people. YES becomes my words, events, beliefs, expectations and voice. All of these combine to influence my voice and the message that I feel led to share with my world.

The Power of NO

I lived YES as a child. It was based upon innocence. We lived out in the country. I played with cousins and friends. We made forts in the woods, dams in the creek and wagons for riding down hills. I knew nothing about death, wars and accidents. I lived in a protected world of love and encouragement.

In 1960, I turned nine, and that summer my father died from pancreatic cancer. He was 48. I was not ready or prepared for him to leave. I expected to spend more time with him as he worked at the shop where I would play—taking imaginary trips pretending to be a bus driver or rolling up the plastic film used to protect windows and making balls. I thought there would be more trips to the store, church and family reunions. My emotionally safe world ended. My heart and spirit hurt in ways I had never known.

His death marked the end of our relationship, but in some ways it signaled the demise of our family. My mother, brother and I continued, but things were different. A year later my mother married again, and this man was not my father nor did he act in a fatherly manner. He was an alcoholic. He struggled with life, and as the only one employed, my mother struggled to keep a roof over our heads and food on the table. There wasn't a sense of family and togetherness. I felt lost and alone. Someone significant had died, and those who were left behind seemed to have wandered away as well.

My father's death introduced me to the concept of NO. Up until this time, *no* was the answer I received for asking about a new toy or a possible visit to a neighbor's house to play. Now, the message was much more troubling. I soon learned that the people you love don't live forever, safety and security can end, and encouragement and support can evaporate.

One of the major truths to emerge from this event for me was that when you lose something you love—whether it is a person, relationship, dream or possession—you hurt. A tornado of pain rips through your heart leaving chaos, debris and unanswered questions. And the pain wasn't limited just to that year. I experienced the grief from his death at every significant moment: turning 16, graduating from high school and college, getting married, having children and now grandchildren. I wanted so much to hear his words of approval and acceptance as the milestones passed, but there was only silence. No one spoke the words I needed to hear from him.

I had grandparents who had died, but it didn't seem to be that difficult of an experience. There was an emotional distance or buffer that insulated me from the pain of their passing. I still had security and support through my parents.

Since the events of 1960, I have learned much about the word NO. I have experienced it in many different forms. It can be the death of loved ones, accident, tornado, flood, fire or resistance to life itself. It can come in many forms. I have found that it can be an internal or external barrier, a boundary that sets limits, a belief, a word that stops action, or an attitude that controls life. It can be demonstrated in a word, event, energy, attitude or belief.

With time, I have discovered that I am not the only person who has faced NO. It happens to people in all walks of life and at every age. NO can be a negative attitude or belief; death of a relationship; end of a life; destruction of a home; loss of faith; shattered dream; failure of a project; or person with self-destructive behavior. It comes with many faces and disguises. It doesn't pretend to offer a lot of consolation. It just stands in the middle of the road with uplifted hand and shouts, "Stop!" All of our hopes, dreams and plans screech to a halt.

Over time, NO can become a language as well. After the storm hits and life settles back down to a new normal, we come to realize that what we had wanted or dreamed of has ended. Things will never be the same again. The pain lingers. We face the prospect of living life without. Hope takes a hit. Faith stumbles. Love shrinks. We question and doubt and wonder what might have been but wasn't. NO then becomes the language of the defeated, lost and uncertain. Something other than a person or relationship has ended. We have lost part of ourselves, and it is reflected in the way we talk, act and think. Our words are no longer filled with the energy and enthusiasm they held previously. A part of us withers on the vine of life under the heat of adversity.

As a minister, I have walked with so many people in their time of NO. Their events are too many to list and too private to share in print, but I have done it enough to speak with certainty—NO, is a difficult experience. The scale varies so much. It can range from a parent denying a request to go out for pizza with a friend to the loss of a loved one, to disease or an accident. The higher the event goes up the scale of life, the more difficult it is to process and the longer it takes to recover.

Used Words

We want the promise of YES. We get the disruption of NO. Now, we live in the gap where these two worlds collide. We are prepared to celebrate the former, but not the latter. One brings baggage that we did not anticipate or want. To survive, we hold on as tightly as a child grasping his favorite stuffed animal in the middle of the night.

We try to explain life to ourselves and others. Searching as diligently as we might look for a set of lost keys, we try to find words—ones that will explain, resolve and fix the situation. We rummage through a stack of them piled up at the back door of our existence. But we can't locate a single one; all are used; some are inherited; some are borrowed; some just don't make sense at all and need to be thrown out with the trash as worn-out vocabulary.

All words are used before they get to us. Someone else wore them before they appeared in our closet. A family member, friend or acquaintance tried them and walked around in them awhile before they got to us. If they did a good job of it, we get it. We find the content, meaning and support we need to survive. If they didn't do well, then we struggle because the words shipped arrive as empty boxes—taped up, ready to open, but empty with nothing in them.

I remember a time when I was in the eighth grade and I really wanted a pair of brown penny loafers for Christmas. I hinted. I suggested. I begged for them. I became curious and started to look in closets around the house to see if Mom had caught the hint—not that she could have missed it. Soon I found the box and opened it. There they were—bright, shiny and new—smelled like new leather. I gently tried them on to make sure they were a good fit. I put them back in the box, careful to fold the tissue paper in the right places. A few days later, I began to wonder how the shoes were doing, so I went back and tried them on again, and again and again. By the time Christmas arrived, there were significant creases across the top where I had walked around the room, and my mother noticed. Likewise, our words show the signs of age and wear in our many efforts to check the fit with who we are and what we face.

We inherit some words from others. I think each family possesses words that are special to them. These may be positive or negative ones. Education was an important one to my father's family, so many of the children entered the teaching profession. *Hate* can become a powerful one when passed down to the third and fourth generation. Families may hate poverty, the causes of it, or the poor people who cross their path. Another one that can be inherited can be *love*. In one family, it may mean hugging, holding and touching, while in another it may mean a stoic, emotionless approach to all relationships. For this reason, even our words need to be examined if we are to ever learn—How Can I Live YES in a NO World?

We live in the gap between "what is" and "what might have been." In this valley between the two hills of YES and NO lie hope, dreams, disappointment, hurt, loss, possibility, fear, potential, freedom, healing, yearning, desire, growth and change. It is where our dreams for life ended and our opportunity for growth begins. But we aren't ready yet; we want to wait; we want to spend more time getting settled here; we want time to pass; we don't want to change; and we want new words to come. Unfortunately, all we can find are used ones—cast aside like empty cereal boxes—but we desperately look through each one hoping to find a morsel of nourishment for our tired and weary spirits.

In my experience, this is the time for us to discover new words, or maybe I should say, "discover our own words." Rather than living with those that have been worn out by others, inherited from friends or family, borrowed from strangers, maybe it is time we voiced our own. With uncertainty and doubt, we hesitate to speak old, discarded or ill-fitting ones. But when we find our own, when we discover God's Divine YES for our lives, when hurts have been healed, when we see the needs in those around us, then we will speak in a confident voice without fear or hesitation. You are on a journey now. Stay with me for a little while as we learn to walk and speak again with an internal confidence that only He can give.

Sacred Stories

Pleasing People

I need to stop pleasing people—that is my problem. "Let your no be no, and your yes be yes, " (Matthew 5:37). It's easy to say yes, though most of the time, we really would rather say no, but we are not bold enough to put down boundaries. Every yes you say when you really would have rather said no; every time you relent to please others; every time you wanted to place a boundary but didn't and then later resented it, turns many yeses into an "I wish I had said no."
~Jeff Davis

Some Come with Baggage

Like every other word, all yeses are not created equal. We seem to be talking about something besides: "Yes, I brought my insurance card...Yes, I'd like more cornbread...Yes, I've put on some weight." I feel like I have an unstable relationship with yes. At times I say yes out of pressure to please—usually self-imposed, or from guilt or a feeling of obligation. So I'm thinking that yes and no both come with lots of baggage, at least for some of us. One of the ways I am experiencing YES these days is all bound up with the gift of grandparenthood. When I was a mere parent, I am afraid my default answer too many times was no. Granted, sometimes no is the right answer. I'm talking about the times I didn't have enough information to give an answer, but said no. Or the times I said no out of my own fears or fatigue, or, worst of all, when I said no because of unrealistic expectations (mine or some nameless, faceless, possibly imaginary critic).

I feel like my grandchildren are giving me a second chance with yes. From birth, their default answer has been, "Yes!...Yes, I am really listening to you, and I hear what you're saying, and it matters to me...Yes, I think you have a good point!...Yes, you make my heart feel happy...Yes, you are safe here and accepted for just exactly who you are!...Yes, I love you more than all the books in the library, and to the moon and back!" and "Yes, I will love you forever no matter what, and even after I'm gone." Yes feels like a sign of respect to me. Learning to offer ourselves (or our grandchildren) the respect of yes just might begin to spread to the world of work, church or politics.

~Ann Lay Ross

No Time Left

I struggle with yes, because I hate to disappoint others. I have a hard time saying no to anyone other than myself, and in the long run, I hurt myself by stretching my life so thin. Now, I'm to a point where with a wife and four children, I have so many yes commitments that I find myself exhausted at the end of each and every day, and I feel that while it appears that I am helping my children by being their baseball and football coach, I'm actually hurting them—by the time I get done every day, I have no time left to be Daddy!

I'm also shafting my wife, because in serving my children through their sports, I also force her into being "the parent" during all of these practices and games. Then there are the

"outside" commitments such as church, friends and work. All of these things that we say yes *to take time. And even though I think I am pleasing others and "doing good"—as I was always taught to do growing up—in actuality, I'm saying* no *to my wife and children. This is one of my many struggles with* yes.
~**Brian Payton**

If

I was 58 when the pressure became too much. I had spent most of my life believing that by always saying yes *to the needs of others, they would love me. I thought that to be a friend, to be liked, I needed to always say* yes *to what my friends wanted. I thought that if I kept my chin up when things went bad and said to the world "Yes, I'm fine," the world would reply, "What a great person." It turns out there are* good yeses *and* bad yeses.

The first losses came at 17. I lost two very dear loved ones that year, one being my PaPa Junkins. He was the best man I ever knew. His loss was devastating, but I just kept going like nothing had happened. I thought that was what I should do. Then I married young and held on for years to an abusive relationship. I lost all my grandparents, a wonderful mother-in-law, many precious aunts and uncles, and I still kept going like that because that was what was expected of me. No time to grieve. When it got to be too much, I would just work harder and shut myself off. No one loves someone who is weak, right?

It took the loss of my father, putting my mother in a nursing home, and the return and subsequent loss of someone I loved dearly to learn that I simply could not earn love. There were no warning signs. I had been everything that I thought he wanted, but he just walked away. The losses were finally just too much, the pain was no longer bearable, and the sudden overflowing sticky mess of tears came as a violent surprise.

Today I thank God every day for putting the people in my life who have taught me that it is okay to be me; the same people who have taught me that saying no *does not make me weak or any less a friend. They have taught me that I am a cherished addition to their lives just as I am, no changing required. I have learned that no matter what I do, I cannot keep the ones who do not love me for who I am. I've learned to accept and mourn the loss of loved ones when God is ready for them. I've learned most importantly, how to just be me. Now, I can say* yes *to the life I want and things that are important to me without worrying about what others think of me (well, most of the time). Now I can say* no *and take a much needed break without feeling an overwhelming sense of guilt for not stretching myself just a little thinner to meet someone else's needs. I still have a hard time saying* yes *to things that might cause me to get hurt (putting my heart out there), but God and I are working on that. I'm happy as me and I'm finally learning to "color outside the lines." I am a YES in progress.*
    ~Judi Payton

On Taking a Dare

I've always felt like I had been blessed growing up—friends, family, education and church. I never honestly felt like I was in want of anything more than what I had. College began, and I graduated with my psychology degree. I began a second degree in Nursing at a new college in a new location. I was searching for something to complete me—for someone. Most of my friends were getting—or had already gotten—married. Some were already parents. I wanted my turn. I wanted to find my soul mate. I answered YES to a dare from really close friends to try eHarmony in January of 2007. Did I have anything to lose? No! Did I have everything to gain? Yes! I filled out all of the forms and matched up with my best friend, soul mate and partner in life on March 4, 2007. He asked me out on a date, and my answer was, "Yes!"

On August 1, 2007, he asked me to marry him, and my answer was, "Yes, Yes, Yes!" On April 5, 2008, I said the best YES when I said, "I do!" On September 28 of that same year, we discovered that, Yes, we are pregnant! On May 26, 2009, I was able to say, Yes, I'm a mother, to an awesome little boy. In the spring of 2010: Yes, we are selling our first house due to military base changes. Yes, I am following my husband wherever we are needed. On September 20, 2010, I know that I am complete. I look into my husband's eyes as we look over our son and smile at one another. I have found who and what I was searching for—the missing pieces. I am affirmed in the moment we laugh over our inside jokes. I enjoy the quiet moments of just being with him. Am I complete? Yes! I celebrate that he is my YES!

I am grateful God led us to find each other. Together, we are learning and discovering many of the ways he has said YES to us. I am amazed at the way God takes our different pieces and molds them into the person he wants us to be.

~Michelle Clark Davison

Power of Their Own Decisions

Right now, my husband and I have a sophomore in college and a senior in high school. I think that is where we need to be using our yes every day. Not just for the questions about, "Can I go?" or "May I have?" Instead, it is the questions the girls ask about themselves, their choices and their future plans. This is a time in the lives of our children that we are cutting the strings and they are taking flight under the power of their own decisions—a scary endeavor for all of us as parents or children. We have tried to raise them right, but they did not always think we were doing things right. They are using what they have been taught in many new situations, and being able to tell them, "Yes, you have made the right decision," or "Yes, we believe you can do that," is very powerful for them and quite reassuring for me. Sometimes a yes given to one person can be an affirmation for the giver as well.

~**Monica Ducker Semrad**

I Often Wonder

My story involves my sister Patsy. I have to give you a little background: I was a menopause baby for my parents. My oldest sister, Elizabeth, was 20, Patsy, 18, and my youngest sister, Dot, was 16 when I was born. By the time I was 26, both my parents had died, so my sisters became my parents. Patsy and I shared so many similar qualities. She had two sons, no daughters, so we were especially close. Patsy was a 10-year survivor of five open-heart bypass surgeries, and I had been with her all the way. In

121

2002, she had an aortic aneurysm that her doctors began watching, and for three years there wasn't any growth or immediate threat. However, on her checkup in March of 2005, the aneurysm had grown to the level that would require surgery. It was determined she could not handle the abdominal surgery, so we were sent to a major hospital for a consult.

We went for the appointment and heard good news: aneurysm at 5, she was a candidate for repair with stents. So, I said, "Yes, this is good." And we set the date for surgery. No one, including Patsy, doubted my decision because of my medical background. We went on a cruise, made lots of memories together and went to the hospital on October 6 for her surgery. Unfortunately, they were unable to fix the aorta with stents, and in the process she got a tear in her artery because it was so fragile. She never came home from the hospital. I often wonder if I had not had a medical background would I have said yes to the surgery, and would she have been with me longer. Perhaps I should have said that we should just take our chances on a rupture because the surgery is too risky and have our days still ahead. So, I am still not sure about that YES—it breaks my heart still now relating it to you.

~Brenda Pike Oglesby

Daddy's Little Girl

As a little girl growing up in a family with four brothers, I turned out to the one who was Daddy's girl. I was the only girl, but I was just as tough as any of the boys. I hunted, fished, built forts in the woods and everything else the boys and my daddy did. As I grew up, this relationship with my daddy grew to the point where, in college, when we would have a phone conversation, he could finish my sentences. My daddy understood his little girl better than I understood myself lots of times. He could make any situation better—not always telling me what I wanted to hear, mostly what I needed to hear, but making the situation feel better anyway.

He was the one I reached out to when I had a problem, needed advice or just needed to talk. When I was attending Abraham Baldwin Agricultural College, my daddy came often to visit. Howard, my husband now, was among my circle of friends. Daddy liked Howard from the first time he met him. After our group of friends transferred to the University of Georgia, life changed. Howard and I became more than friends. I confided in my daddy the first time Howard kissed me that it was like kissing a brother. Daddy's comment was, "You will get over that," and I did. And we were married within about two years of that first kiss. We have been married for 19 years now.

I knew when he was diagnosed with colon cancer that it was bad, but I expected we would go through the treatments, he'd be really sick, and then he would recover and be around for a while longer. He was only 64, way too young to be going away. I spent every minute I could with him when he was sick. I spent nights in the hospital and went to chemotherapy. We talked until the wee hours of the morning one night when he was in the hospital for what would become the last time I would see him alive.

It was a Thursday night. I went home on Friday with plans to come back on Sunday for my mom's birthday and of course to see my daddy. As I was leaving on Sunday morning, Mama called me and told me not to come by myself, that daddy had to be taken to ICU. I was a wreck. When I got to the hospital, I went up to the floor he was on and Mama told me he was gone. I felt like

123

my world had collapsed around me, I couldn't breathe. I lost it. I could only say, "Oh God, No! No! Why?" He couldn't be gone—not my daddy, my world, my heart. I couldn't believe he was gone, and I hadn't seen him one last time before he died. And my poor mother—he passed away on her birthday...just not fair at all!

When he died seven years ago, a part of my world went away with him. I felt like I would never feel normal again. My daddy hung the moon and stars in my world. There were many dark nights after he was gone. I got mad at God for taking him away. I argued with Him that it wasn't fair. I had friends whose parents had gone through the same illness Daddy had, and they still had their parents. My life was a huge NO at that point. I cried for weeks, mostly by myself; I didn't want to share the pain with anyone else. Howard was so good during this time, so sweet and caring. My children were also. I felt like my heart had completely broken in two, and I knew it would never heal. This was—and is by far—the worst thing I have ever had to endure. There is no way to adequately describe the pain that I felt. My friends were a huge source of strength for me.

Each day that has passed in these last seven years has been a step toward that new normal that I am living. It is still odd to go home to Mama's house and Daddy not be there. I have great memories of our times together and his tender loving ways. He was a big man, 6 feet 2 inches tall, but he was a gentle man too. I see hints of him in my son, Witt, which gives me great comfort. This new normal gets easier every day to adjust to. The ache is still there, but that too is a part of the new normal. That ache will always be there until I get to see him again in perfection in Heaven.

God didn't wait long to give me a chance to use this loss to comfort someone else who lost their daddy too soon. When a good friend lost her daddy the next year, I cried with her and talked to her and assured her that I knew what she was feeling. We now help each other through Father's Day, birthdays, and death anniversaries. She is living in another town now, but we still talk often.

I thank God for her and for giving me someone to comfort so soon after his death. That is also a blessed part of the new normal—using my trial to help someone else through theirs. I now actually get through some days without the pain—just the sweet memories of hunting, walks in the woods, or just the time we spent talking about life, faith, love and family. Those days get more numerous as time goes by. But, there are the days that the ache returns and always will. That is part of the new normal also.

~Kim Allegood Brown

A Season Ticket to a New Beginning

My mother died when she was 49 from breast cancer. I was seven months pregnant at the time and in nursing school. I also had an 8-year-old and a 4-year-old, so my plate was full and running over. I rarely had time to myself with all that I had to do. There was a group of older ladies, that I had known all of my life, who attended our church. They all purchased season tickets to the Macon Theatre each season. For several years, my mother drove this group of ladies to the plays. They didn't like to drive at night, and my mother really enjoyed going with them, though she was much younger. After Mama died, one of the ladies called me and explained that Mama's season ticket was still good and asked me if I would like to finish out the season with them. Of course, I would have to drive them. I said yes, though I had not attended many plays and doubted it was something I would enjoy.

What else could I say? If I said no, there was a possibility that these ladies would miss the rest of the season. My friends couldn't believe that I had taken on another task and truthfully, neither could I! More than once they asked me if I had lost my mind. What had I done? As it turns out, I drove the ladies to the play for 10 years. It wasn't always easy, and there were years that I truly thought would have to be my last, as my responsibilities and children grew. I had to find a babysitter at times, rush to get off work, and was usually exhausted, but I only missed taking them one time during those years. We all went through so much during that time. I graduated from nursing school, took on a new job, raised children, divorced and remarried. Through each event, they offered gracious support and encouragement.

And their families and lives changed too—graduations, new grandbabies or great grandbabies, marriages, divorces, deaths. Eventually, one by one, each lady dropped out for various reasons, usually health related, and some have passed away. But each year as the season's end approached, they would ask if I would like to go one more year, and every year I said YES! They always purchased my ticket and took turns paying for my meal. I provided the car and the gas. Because of this deal, they were able to attend the plays, but I received so much more. Sharing an evening with women from all walks of life, at least two generations older than I was, is something I will never forget. We enjoyed the meal, critiqued the plays and shared much laughter. Their kindness, tact, and politeness towards me and each other, is something we just don't experience very often, these days. There is a memorial service for one of my ladies this Saturday, and I am sure that as I sit there at her service, I will reflect on my special time with her and the rest of our friends. Losing each lady has been hard and though saying YES to them year after year was difficult at times, now I wish I could say YES to them just one more time.

   ~Melissa Jones Mitchell

Reflections

Over a lifetime, many people enter and leave our lives. If wisdom could be manufactured and passed along, we would have been able to recognize the significance of each one. We would have spent more time, valued meaningful moments, and stored up special memories with the people in our world that would have lasted a lifetime. We didn't know. We can only hold onto what remains.

Some leave too soon. An accident, disease or personal struggle takes people away from us before we are ready for them to go. The relationship didn't end. The person just left— by their own decision or unexplained reason.

Some stay too long. People can be toxic. They aren't healthy. They have not addressed or worked through their deeper issues. Some are mentally unstable. They linger— creating an ongoing emotional virus that keeps us on the verge of sickness. We would like for them to go away, but they don't.

With each one, we gain and we lose. With every gift, there is a good side and a not-so- good side. Embrace the goodness of each person who has entered your life. You didn't create them. Listen for the positive that they bring. Be aware of the negative, but do not be consumed by their limitations.

This process of growing and learning helps us teach our gatekeepers when to open and close. Without being assigned a purpose or power, those imaginary doors allow anyone and anything to consume our time and life.

Through these entrances and exits, we have heard the hint of God's YES and NO for us. The powers of these words develop over time and with each new experience. You are someone else's YES. You are someone else's NO. Continue to walk the path into the pain and through to healing. Your word is waiting for you to discover it.

Wounded Spirits

Prayer for Wounded Spirits

Heavenly Father,

Our spirits are wounded. We thought we were "stepping up to the plate" to hit a slow pitch; instead we have had curves, fast balls and wild pitches bouncing in every direction. The twists and turns of life have come at us pretty hard. Our hearts carry hurt. Some of the wounds go down to the very depth of our soul. We wanted a pain-free journey. We have been whacked and knocked around by the unexpected. We believe you are with us, but we sometimes wonder. How could a loving God allow such a bad thing to happen—to us?

It seems that the pain surrounds and overwhelms. We walk on but without a lot of confidence. Allow us to accept the gift of life —the joy and pleasure as well as the pain and sorrow. You invite us to, "Come unto me all who are burdened and heavy laden," so that we might receive the promise of "rest." These words tug at our hearts to let go and trust again. The pain holds on tight to our spirit. We yearn for a new day. We are searching for a peace of mind that doesn't just provide an end to the hurt but will lead us to a day of new beginnings. O' God, we want to find a resting place—O' God, we want to find a home.

In Christ's Name,

Amen

A Difficult Relationship

Adversity comes along like some giant alien from a "B" movie and knocks us off our highway to happiness. We have a dream. We have a wish for the future. As Karen Jones Richardson describes, we have "an unconscious contract with God" that our lives will go well.

So we get married with the dream that we will stay together forever, but divorce comes along and ends the relationship. We have children, expecting that they will grow up to become the above-average person we know they will be, but they make poor choices, and they go in a different direction. We work to develop a career that will lead to retirement and enjoyment of all of the pleasures we have imagined, but the company downsizes the workforce. We move to new locations so that we can find the happiness we didn't have at the last place we called home only to discover we face the same challenges.

It is difficult to define our relationship to adversity. You can't really call it *a friend,* because friends don't hurt those they love. You can't call it *an enemy,* though it can destroy your confidence and peace. You can't say that it is spiritual, though some will suggest God allows it to take place to teach us lessons that we need to learn.

Because we can't define our relationship with it, we struggle coming to grips with how to cope, trust and live through the tough times. If bad things happen because God allows them to occur, then life becomes very random. Some individuals are selected for deep pain and suffering; others enjoy success and affluence.

I have experienced a few difficult moments along the way. The death of parents and grandparents, a house fire, automobile accidents, family moves, surgeries, mid-life crisis, and a laundry list of lesser life events have dotted the landscape of my existence. But what do you do with them? Or, better still, what do I let them do to me? Do I set up a pity party for me? Do I hold them up as trophies to illustrate the pain that has been endured? Or, share them as reasons for why I can't move forward or live productively? Some people might suggest that these point out the randomness and unpredictability of how things happen.

As a minister, I have walked with individuals through some really tough situations. Murder, accidents, suicide, death of loved ones, tornadoes, house fires, loss of job, divorce, addiction, and a long list of other experiences plague people on a daily basis. With over thirty years of going through the shadows with others, my mind and heart have been opened to understand how the human spirit struggles with setbacks. I offer some reflections on what I have I observed when I see someone facing life's difficult moments.

It comes unexpectedly. Adversity never phones ahead, nor does it send out a notice. It simply arrives one day and knocks on the door of your life.

It shows no respect to person, status or location. Neither tornadoes nor hurricanes pay much attention to the address on the house. Weather conditions come together to create an act of nature that blows through the lives of those that are impacted while leaving others a few feet away untouched. There is no difference—whether you live in a mansion or a lean-to—when your home has been destroyed. It is still your home. It is your place, no matter the size, shape, color or location.

It comes in different forms. Death, divorce, flat tires, and lost car keys all fall under the heading of *difficult moments.* As you can imagine, some impact us more than others.

It affects everyone. From Main Street to the boardroom, life happens.

It strips away the superficial. When the tough times come, anything artificial is immediately useless. Priorities shift. Instantly you see what is important and what is no longer of value.

It teaches the deeper truths of life. Some lessons are never learned without adversity. We get in a routine and life moves on autopilot. You don't slow down or stop to enjoy people and moments of reflection. When bad stuff happens, we go to another speed. It is the one without pretense, roles or positions. It is the one where people speak from their pain and listen with their ears of compassion. A relationship develops that bonds people together in ways that are difficult to understand.

It changes us. I think adversity wounds us in many ways. Emotions surface because we are disappointed and we experience loss. We hurt. We feel the pain of damaged relationships, opportunities and dreams. I believe that one of the deepest hurts that may occur is to our faith. We look around for an explanation for why bad things happen and can easily slide into the belief that God made it take place. Then it is one small step to the idea that God looked away and wasn't paying attention. Therefore, I can't trust God. I do understand how easily this can take place. For other individuals, their trust becomes more real. Their faith is refined by the fires of adversity, and it is stripped of anything other than a simple trust that there is a presence and strength that goes beyond any other relationship.

A Simple Thought

Here is a brief theological point of view. I believe that the Creator of the universe granted freedom to everything that exists. It was built into the blueprint of life. This grants people the opportunity to make choices and exercise their power in the course or direction of what takes place in their world. This same freedom was granted for all creation according to its kind. Each facet of existence was blessed with freedom and power to pursue its purpose.

In this design of freedom, life becomes more unpredictable and random. The divine creator isn't located on a celestial cloud pushing buttons and watching people squirm or jump. So where is he? For me the answer is in Christ. The Gospel of John reads (John 1: 1, New International Verion), "In the beginning was the Word and the Word was with God and the Word was God." God became incarnate in Christ that we might understand his true nature. It is the desire to be with us.

Adversity happens because life happens. It takes place according to the laws of nature.

So, what do I do with adversity? It becomes a companion to my experience. It becomes my teacher. I ask it questions. I listen. I walk into it. I listen to what is being said about me and my existence. I pay attention. I allow it to help me learn deeper truths. I let the pain flow over, around and through me. I let it carry me to a new place; a different place than where I started.

I allow it to help me let go of the superficial and search for permanent truths. I become a student of my own loss, grief and struggle. I ask God to walk with me; stand with me; give me strength; help me hurt; hold me in his arms of Grace; accept me as a broken person; let his strength shine through my limitations; and give me the opportunity for a second, third, or fourth chance to start over again. For I live, as one store suggests, in "The Do-Over Place" all of the time. I learn that life isn't so much about the destination as much as it is about being present in each and every moment so that I can embrace the gift of the sacred in looking into my wife's eyes, sharing a meal with a friend, holding my grandchildren's hands, or sitting with someone who has lost a loved one and know that these are the gifts of life.

Knocked Off the Road

On the good days, life is tough. Wrapped up as a great, big unopened present, it seems to hold constant surprise regarding what may spring out of the box at any given moment. Forrest Gump stated that, "Momma always said life is like a box of chocolates. You never know what you're going to get."

I see it more as a jigsaw puzzle. The picture on the cover doesn't always match the pieces on the inside. We can gripe and groan about the broken expectation, or we can get to work building the best picture we can with the pieces that are left. With time you can find satisfaction in putting together a variety of pictures from one box whether it matches the one that you thought would be there or not.

One Friday morning in the spring of 2000, I left for a business meeting in a city about 50 miles away from my home. When I arrived at the interstate, I turned into the entrance ramp and accelerated to merge into the flow of cars and trucks. I moved into a gap in the traffic in the nearest lane. As I drove down a long hill, an 18-wheeler passed my car in the middle lane. We reached the lowest point traveling side-by-side and then began going up the rise of another hill. Gravity slowed the truck and I began to pull up even, first with the trailer and then the cab. As my front window moved parallel with the front bumper of the truck, I suddenly felt the sensation of "this truck is going to hit me." And it did. I had moved into the driver's blind spot, he swerved to the right and smacked my car while we both traveled at 70 mph. My car fish-tailed and then skidded broadside in front of his truck. A thought entered my mind that was so innocent and empty of fear: "So this is how I am going to die." I didn't...as he continued to push my spinning car across the other lanes of the interstate until it slid to a stop in the median. The car was demolished. I had a few bruises and scratches, but nothing more.

As the highway patrolman stated, "It just wasn't your time to go." I was lucky.

I was in the driver's blind spot on that day, and I got hit. This took place on an interstate. Most of my whacks haven't been on a highway; they have been ones that have come from people that have left me with some bent emotional fenders or crunched spirit—the kind of damage you can't send to a repair shop or expect to get fixed in 10 days or less.

Life's Blind Spots

Sometimes it feels like we get caught in the blind spot of life as well. We get whacked, smacked and punched around pretty hard by something that comes our way. Kim Brown, a friend, put it in these words, "We get knocked off of the road, through the ditch, and over the cliff."

Pick up any small town newspaper and browse through it over the course of a few days, and you will read the stories of lives that have been changed by an unexpected event. Why? Adversity comes knocking on the door of every life on a regular basis.

After Shock

I don't think as many problems result from the knocks as from what happens after we get up and try to walk around again. We know that a hurtful event can happen at any point in time. The real anguish begins when we feel the aftershock of loss, hurt and grief over the life we might have had. This is where I think we lose our hopes and dreams for what might have been. I would call these *our secondary losses*.

You might think the event that hit you is the most important piece. It isn't. The bent fenders and bumpers are surface stuff. It is the emotional trauma that comes from any major life experience that holds the most lasting effect. Why? It is hidden underneath the surface of our lives where only we see, notice and feel the lingering impact. We carry the silent pain every day and moment of our existence.

Most of the emotional pain I experienced as a child was formed within a five-year period of time. From age 8-13, a series of events took place that robbed me, to some degree, of my childhood, innocence and security. My world changed from one of fun, laughter and safety to one of hurt, loss and uncertainty.

Friends and family who knew me at the time will be surprised to read these words. From a distance, they would have seen the chaos, but would not have known the details— and they shouldn't. For one lesson I learned early in life was to be a good boy. You might think this would mean always be polite, courteous, obedient and considerate of others. And I was. I always have been.

My father's recovery from surgery became an extended hospital stay. It lasted about two months until he died. Our daily routine was the same: get up, go to the hospital, spend the day there, and come home after supper. Often, I was farmed out to stay with family members or friends. Hospitals and 9-year-old boys are not a good combination. You can look under soft drink machines for change, walk up and down the halls, visit the patients you know, and explore the grounds outside the building only so many times... then you get bored.

I was at the hospital sitting with my dad one day when he asked me to come up to the side of his hospital bed. My mother had left the room to run an errand, and my brother was away at college. I was sitting doing nothing. He said, "Randy, come here for a minute," and I did. He slipped his arm around my shoulders and pulled me close. Then he began to share, "You know I have been sick for a while. One day I will get better. When I do, I want to take you fishing. Would you like to do that? Also, I want you to always remember you are Daddy's little boy. I want you to grow up to be a good boy. You will won't you?" Those are the last words I remember my dad saying to me. I know there were others as I came for a visit or left for the day, but these were significant words.

I don't know if he knew he was dying or not at the time. My guess is that he did. Unknowingly, an emotional contract was formed that day: I would always be a good boy. No one told me what that meant. I wasn't instructed in how to be a good person. I figured it out on my own as I picked up on the signals from the adults around me. My interpretation of what good boys do has evolved over the years: maintain emotional control so that you don't upset those around you: always be kind, considerate, and respectful; do your work and do it well; make other people happy; put their needs first; sacrifice so others will have life easier. There are some additional thoughts, but these are the main ones.

This ghost of a relationship has lingered and been both a curse and blessing. The blessing has been that I have always tried to be likeable. I mean, why not? The curse may be larger though. You are nice whether you want to be or not. Also, you put the needs of others above your own to the point you may not ever live out your own purpose for being here.

Someone Wasn't Paying Attention

There is another wound that emerged from this same period of time in my life. It was one to the spirit.

My parents were good people. They were hard-working, church-going, and fun-loving people. We went to Poplar Log Freewill Baptist Church. There was Sunday School, worship, revivals, and decorations. Families came together. We read, we prayed, we worshiped. We sought to be faithful.

When my dad became sick, the focus of our family was on his survival and ours as well. When he died, my mother remarried a year later. Survival surfaced in another form. My stepfather was an alcoholic. He struggled to stay sober and even keep a job. He didn't do well with either of these. That left my mother as the sole bread-winner and means of support for our family. She did the best she could. Putting food on the table was a higher priority than anything else.

During all of this change, hurt, loss and pain, no one ever sat down with me and talked about what was taking place— how to deal with it or how to process the grief. It got stored away in the good-boy's closet where it stayed fed and kept alive over the years with additional setbacks or disappointments.

I don't share these stories for your pity or to create sadness for you, but for reflection. As I look back now, it seems the sensation I have most often felt is that no one was paying attention. My dad was too busy trying to deal with his health and facing the prospect of imminent death. My mother was left as a single mother needing to create income to care for two boys, a 100-acre farm and fulltime expenses. She was too busy trying to survive... but in a different kind of way.

Now, I think I can see the deeper issue that we face with adversity and getting knocked around by life. Or, maybe I should say, "I see more clearly where I have struggled." It is the unspoken belief that God was not paying attention to my life. If we are good people, we embrace faith, strive to be obedient and seek to live in a way that reflects those values. Then when we get hit by a major life event we look around say, "Hey, wait a minute. What just happened? I am good. I am faithful. I am a believer. And this has turned my world upside down. Okay, God this wasn't in the contract." A shorter response might be, "Where were you God when I needed you the most?"

I don't think we just get hit, knocked or smacked. I think our lives feel the repercussion to the core of our being. Our life was planned. There was a roadmap leading to happiness, success and contentment. Then something happened. We get hurt physically and emotionally. Our souls are wounded because we cannot put the pieces back together again the way it used to be. We want to rewind the clock, but we can't. And our souls hurt, because we lost something we loved. We lost our sense of God in our lives.

Uncharted Territory

Falling off the Map

Maps are obsolete. We don't use them much anymore. On rare occasions when the GPS doesn't work, or you have to make do in finding your direction, we might open up the trunk of the car in hopes that an old atlas or state map might have been tossed in there for safe keeping.

Maps serve a useful purpose in visualizing how we see our lives. You have stood at the entrance to a mall looking at the directory layout, and there you see the small words, "You are here." This helps you find your current location. You can then make decisions about which turns to take to get to your next shopping or dining opportunity.

Most of us born in America come pre-programmed with a destination in mind. We are headed toward happiness, success and financial well-being. I forgot to add: with our family loving, supporting, and encouraging us every step of the way. This untested secret code creates major problems when we get knocked around by life. You still know who you are. You are clear on your name, age and ambition for life. Yet, something is very different. We don't know how to navigate adversity well. This uncharted storm causes uncertainty, false steps and a desire for quick relief.

Basically, we don't have a way to integrate storms and adversity into our lives. These events happen on the news and to other people, but not us. So, when they do occur, we get lost. Our plans are clear, our lives are set. Adversity necessitates an adjustment to our planned course, and we don't want to make it.

Standing on Shaky Faith

We are a people of faith. All of us are. Some will say they have no faith, but they really do. They have a faith that nothing exists. So they trust their own wisdom and experience more than they do any other source. They may not realize that even the ability to doubt and question is a gift of faith. You have to doubt something. That something has to be out there for us to ever disagree with it.

When adversity strikes, our faith takes a hit. It creates an earthquake of the spirit. Our souls shake. The bigger the event, the more it impacts who we are. The structures we have built—family, work, home and well-being—are traumatized. Our faith becomes a little shaky. Some who have prayed stop praying altogether. Others pull back from their support system and try to make it on their own.

Searching for Answers

We try to find an explanation for what has taken place and make sense out of all of the mess. Because we want to explain why a bad event happened, we look at ourselves first. Maybe we were bad, disobedient, critical or whatever else we see as a negative tendency in our lives.

Then friends and family offer ideas. This is where you begin to encounter the common thinking of the day. Answers vary but usually fall somewhere close to one of these:

- It was God's will.
- There is a reason.
- We will understand it one day.
- It is making you stronger.
- They are in a better place.
- They are in heaven.

The sad part about all of these answers is I don't have to make these up. These come from real conversations that I have stored away over the years.

Help or Hurt

A friend shared, "When we lost our little girl at 21 weeks gestation, we were devastated. The most meaningful and helpful encounters were the hugs. Just hold on to me; don't try to find any words to make it better, because there are none. The most hurtful was when a well-meaning individual called to tell me that God has a way of aborting things that were never meant to be. It's been seven years, and I still struggle with that comment."

There are plenty of people who simply come, stand with you, hold you for a while and give you space. These will be your biggest sources of strength and support. Unfortunately, it only takes a few ill-advised words to make the pain last longer than needed.

At this point, I think we try to move too quickly to explain life. We want the pieces to make sense and fit together into a neat cohesive whole, and they don't. But we try to force the pieces into spaces so that the puzzle will make sense again and everything will get back to normal.

Holding the tension

A friend, Angee Knight McKee, shared these words: "When I faced a particularly challenging situation, a good friend told me to, "Hold the tension." In other words, don't be so quick to act to fix things. Wait quietly, listen, discern, *then* act. Hold the tension—your desire to jump into action or reaction. When adversity strikes, we want it to stop or end. We want peace and harmony. We don't want to hurt nor do we want the pain to continue. So we search for a reason this thing took place. We move quickly to fix the situation. In doing so, we miss the most valuable lesson of all. And that is our life.

You don't fix a life. You live it. When it gets broken by adversity, setback or pain, you walk with the pain long enough to decide what steps you can take at this time with the energy and strength you have available. You get down in the ditch where the mess happened. You get oily, greasy and dirty. You start looking for a way to put together the pieces.

No one is really a good life mechanic. You can't take classes on how to fix your life in 10 minutes or less, yet that is what we all want. We look for the "instant answer, quick fix, or immediate relief solution," and those are just not out there.

When do we get in the most trouble helping others or ourselves? When we pretend to have the answer, when we think we know God's will, when we act like we care, and when we go on like nothing ever happened. We try to hand people band-aids when they have injuries that threaten their spirits.

I am calling this your YES. This is the time we get real, get dirty, and get ready to do the tough work of helping ourselves and others heal their souls. It is recognizing the adversity, facing the pain, accepting the broken expectations, and leaning into a different version of me—one slow methodical step at a time. You don't crash your car then jump right back in it and try to enter a drag race. You don't crash your life then jump right back up and try to run a marathon.

Answering the Third Question

When our lives are disrupted by adversity, the first question that we ask is, "What just hit me?" It is a good one. This gives us time to look at the damage and evaluate what happened. It is designed to protect us. So, initially we may live in a state of shock for a few days. This is an emotional capsule that offers some protection until we have time to come to grips with what took place.

Stuck at the Four-Way Stop

The second question that always follows is, "Why did this happen to me?" I call this *The Eternal Why.* Everyone asks it. Someone loses a loved one, and they ask, "Why me?" Another person faces a series of medical tests and receives a negative report, and the question that will always be asked is, "Why?" It is our nature to want to understand the dynamic of life. Having an explanation seems to make the situation and pain more bearable. If we can just explain it to ourselves then maybe the adversity will make sense.

Unfortunately, asking the *why* question keeps us stuck at the four-way stop. We become locked at the scene of the accident. We want to stay there and replay what happened, who hit us, and how bad the damage might be. We do need to stay in place long enough to heal. Depending upon the intensity and duration of the adversity, it can take a very long time.

If we don't heal, then we may become emotionally paralyzed. Staying at the scene of the event—if we are not careful—can lead to an ongoing "pity party of pain." Every time someone drives by, we want to flag them down and let

149

them look at the movie of what just took place in our life. We then become more focused on replaying the video than we do in healing and moving forward.

I also see it another way. Imagine that we go on a fieldtrip to a carnival. You remember there are lots of choices for food, rides and games, but suppose that as we enter, we decide to ride the merry-go-round. We give the attendant our ticket, climb up on one of the horses, and began to ride round and round... and round. As we go in one big circle after another and the horses glide up and down the poles, we begin to notice that the scenery is all the same. The same faces look at you. You don't make any progress other than going in a circle. To me this is like asking the *why* question—it keeps you locked into the same scenery, answers and emotional state. In the end, it isn't one that anyone can completely answer.

As a minister, I have had an untold number of people look me in the eye and ask, "Why did this happen?" In an effort to respond to a broken heart, I have been tempted to offer a superficial answer. But in the deepest part of my being I cannot say, "This was God's will." I don't think it is God's will for a baby to be stillborn or to die a few days later with a birth defect. I don't think it is God's will for children to be killed in accidents or die from cancer. I don't think it is God's will for people to take their own lives or gun down others over a pack of cigarettes or a few dollar bills.

I have also learned that I can't explain the ways of God or natural disaster. Instead, I have questions. I think we would do well to sit with them for a while to see what we can learn about ourselves and our lives.

Sitting with a Good Question

For this reason, I must ask other questions. I must ask more than *what* and *why*. At the four-way stop of life, there are many other roads to take. I can't stay stuck or stalled with just one word.

I do realize you cannot move too quickly. Time is needed to hurt, and time is needed to heal. Time is needed for the recovery of body, mind, spirit and emotions to take place. Common wisdom will often say, "Time heals all wounds." I don't think so.

At least it hadn't healed the broken heart of a mother I met in New York who lost one of her four children in an accident with a drunken driver 18 years earlier. In her words, "It is as painful today as it was then."

We can't depend on time any more than we can find healing in common wisdom. Maybe there is another direction to consider. There is value in knowing when to ask a new question and to sit with it for a while so that it may teach you new truths that are yet to be discovered.

In his blog, "The Healing Path," P. Ryan Ball shares a quote from the writings of "Letters to a Young Poet" that has made me pause for a while.

> *...I would like to beg you dear Sir, as well as I can, to have patience with everything unresolved in your heart and to try to love the questions themselves as if they were locked rooms or books written in a very foreign language. Don't search for the answers, which could not be given to you now, because you would not be able to live them. And the point is to live everything. Live the questions now. Perhaps then, someday far in the future, you will gradually, without even noticing it, live your way into the answer.*[x]

With this thought, Mr. Ball goes on to share some of his personal journey. I find it intriguing because he puts into words what I am trying to communicate.

One question that I live with is this: Why do I have cerebral palsy?

Here's what I know: I have cerebral palsy. Why? I'm not so sure. But I think that's the wrong question anyway.

Here's the right question: Knowing I have cerebral palsy, how shall I live?

Patiently–with wonder and with gratitude–I am living that question. I am living many others, too. Perhaps one day I will live my way into the answer. But I'm not counting on it. The wonder of living these questions is satisfying enough. Continue walking down this path toward healing with these sacred questions in your hands. Live the questions. Consider as a gift any signposts we may encounter along the way, but otherwise be content with the journey. ^{xi}

As long as we are asking *why*, we are dealing with issues we cannot answer. We are stuck. We are paralyzed by a situation we cannot reverse, change or undo. Instead, maybe we should hold the question in our hearts for a while. Treat it as a trust to be protected and treasured. And then change the question. Instead of asking, "Why did this happen?" maybe we should ask, "How can I live now that this event or experience has entered my life?"

I love the way Mr. Ball suggests that we may "...live our way into the answer."

Moving to Another Layer

On a recent visit to Disney World in Orlando, Fla., my daughter, son-in-law and grandson scheduled a backstage tour. This enabled them to see how the world of Disney operates behind the scenes so that all visitors can enjoy an uninterrupted experience of fun. It seems that all of the parks are designed in layers. The top level is where visitors move from one theme park to another, enjoy the rides and special events and eat at many of the restaurants or snack shops. On the lower level, there is a series of tunnels that allow characters and employees to move from one part of the park to the other without being seen or creating a distraction. This free-flow of small vehicles or golf carts allows services to be delivered and employees to move around without disrupting guests.

When I heard their description of their experience, I realized this is what I wanted to visualize for others. Most of life seems to be lived on the top level. There are births and babies, children and families, birthdays, graduations, weddings and retirements. All of our life is engaged in the scenery, seasons, sections, and "Magic Kingdom" of life as we travel toward our destination of happiness or success.

Adversity strikes, and while everything stays the same, it is different. All things are still in place, but I have changed. Old answers don't fit new questions. I am not content when someone says to me, "The truck changed lanes and hit you." I can't hear, "It was God's will." I am not open to those who suggest, "I am sure there is a reason." These don't work. They don't fit. I am not satisfied. I want more. My spirit hungers and thirsts for a different source of nourishment. I want one that gives me back some meaning and purpose for being alive. I cannot find it in conventional wisdom or scripture-of-the-day responses.

This desire for more is where I think our second YES for life begins. Our first YES was one of hopes, dreams, potentials and possibilities. It opened wide the door to all of life. Yet, in our excitement and enthusiasm, we overlooked, or maybe failed to see, the sign off to the side that read, "Door just opened to another direction in life." And we definitely didn't read the fine print that stated, "Whether you wanted it or not."

For this reason, I think our pathway to YES again leads straight into the pain. Like one of the old Tarzan movies where there is a large river ahead, you can't walk around it and you can't swing over it. You have to walk into it.

Walking into the Pain

On a recent cross-state roadtrip, my wife and I noticed that our windshield became dirtier and dirtier with each long mile. Bugs, dirt and pollen added layers of grime that made it difficult to see the road in front of us. As long as I focused on the grunge on the windshield I could not see clearly. But if I looked *through* the glass, I could still see all of the highway and road signs that I needed for driving.

The problem is one that we all face when it comes to pain. We look *at* the events and hurt because that is what has impacted us the most. We don't often step back and try to look *through* the pain to see what might lie beyond and to see what hasn't changed that allows us to continue.

YES Comes with Baggage

I like the way my friend Ann Ross, states it, "So I'm thinking that YES and NO both come with lots of "baggage," at least for some of us."

It does come with baggage. For when we say YES, we are saying it to all of life. A big door swings wide open and there in front of us lies a whole array of experiences, like unopened packages. There is love and joy, happiness and contentment, peace and harmony and so many more positive qualities waiting to be discovered. We fail to realize or consider that when you say YES to one part of life you are saying YES to all of it. So if we embrace love, then we have to recognize hate. If we want happiness, we face the reality of sadness. If we accept the gift of a relationship, we must consider that the relationship may end.

This isn't a pleasant thought, yet it is there. We want marriage, but there may be divorce. We want children, but there could be infertility. We look for success but may find disappointment. We want potential but run the risk of disaster. You really can't have one aspect of life without the other. With the positive comes the negative. When we say YES, we must also accept NO. Without this tension, there wouldn't be a lot of energy, passion or potential. With it, there is risk, uncertainty and unpredictability.

Then pain enters the picture as an uninvited guest. No one sent out a note or requested his attendance, but there he is. So, we act surprised that he would show up. He strolled up to the front door of our life, walked right into our den and sat down in our favorite chair.

Pain is a signal that something significant has taken place. Someone I loved has died. A relationship I valued has ended. A dream I held has been shattered. A child I protected has been harmed. Pain lets me know I have lost something important to me. The bigger the loss has been, the bigger the pain will be. The bigger the pain has been, the longer it will take to heal. In and of itself, pain is neutral. It doesn't sit off in some hidden cave randomly looking at street or phone numbers waiting for the Friday night lottery to pull the winning ticket out of the hat and then go stay with a family for awhile.

Recognizing the Sacred Gift

I would suggest that pain is a gift. It lets us know we are alive. It tells us we have loved. It reminds us that there is something more to life than our plans. We stand where the veil between this world and the next one becomes very thin. We can almost make out the outline of someone walking past the curtain on the other side of the window, but not quite. Pain stops us in our tracks. It causes us to halt all plans and activities.

It is a gift because life is sacred. It is a mystery we can't completely get our heads or hearts around. About the time we think we have nailed this thing down with some big, long nails of certainty, along comes an earthquake or tsunami, and we go back to square one. We stand with parents in the delivery, witness the miracle of birth, and know we have seen a miracle. We wait with family members as a loved one slips away to the other side, and we know we have seen another miracle. Yet, I wonder why we only use words like *miracle* and *sacred* for birth or death?

So, what is my point, you may ask? Don't waste the pain. Don't let this life experience that you don't want and really try to resist slip away from you into the dark alley never to be seen again. Sit with it for a while. Lean into the hurt. Let it hold you in its arms. When we hurt we want to walk faster—almost run—to get away from the source of the pain. I am not sure that is the best thing to do. Instead, I would suggest we slow down, let it walk with us for awhile, and let it speak to us the truths we will never learn without these moments together.

As I have listened to my life, I now can describe to you the people, places and events where pain entered my life. For many years, these became shrines of pity to me. I would go to them often and bow down to worship them as some gods of life. These were the signs that I had lived a tough life. Who hasn't? What that really meant was that I was stuck. My life was frozen stiff by events that had happened years and years ago. I couldn't completely embrace the present moment, because parts of me were still paralyzed by the past. I couldn't completely look forward to the future, because some hurt from the past was still renting space in my heart and emotions.

Permission for Transformation

It seems to me that if you don't walk into the pain then it holds you hostage. You are forever stuck in the past. I grew up and aged, but a lot of my emotional wellbeing was hung up in the time when my dad died.

To get out of this prison, requires transformation. You can't act or live like a captive any longer. Some don't want to leave the pain behind. It has become the norm for them. They are well acquainted with the bars, locks and cells of existence. In a twisted kind of way, the pain becomes a badge of being a victim. Life hit hard. I hurt. Now, see how bad I feel. There is a badge that, in some cases, we wear with pride. To leave this confining space, requires courage and vulnerability. You have to be honest about the experience that hit you and find ways to move forward with a different version of you.

I don't want to suggest—nor do I want you to hear—that I believe pain is a simple little process to master. It is neutral. It is a noun. It is the great teacher of life. It stops us in our tracks. It strips away pretense and artificiality. It shows no respect for where you live, what your level of education might be, what assets you hold or what goals you have set. It isn't easy.

Yet, it is the ultimate transformer. After you have lived with pain, your priorities are realigned, and not only do you want to do things differently, you are a different person. There now are wounds and scars, hurt and healing, and brokenness and wholeness, because there is a new version of you evolving out of the pieces. You keep the best from the past and recreate who you are for a new future.

Lessons from Oz

"The Wizard of Oz[xii]" provides many lessons on transforming life. Dorothy begins the story as an immature, unappreciated young lady. She ends the story by becoming a young woman who recognizes the value of people and the place she called *home*. In a sense, we are all going through Oz on our way to not only our physical home but the sense of home we want to create in this world for ourselves and others.

I have selected five themes intentionally. I believe these are ones that relate to healing and wholeness. These are not the only lessons to be learned—there are so many more—but for the purpose of this book, I have limited my choices to five. Read them. Listen to them. Sit with each thought for a while. See what each one tells you about the movie and your life.

Everyone Gets Blown Out of Kansas

I remember the first time I saw "The Wizard of Oz." I was mesmerized. Every color, character and event jumped from the screen to become permanently embedded in my memory.

Most can relate to what Dorothy experienced—her frustrations with people that led to her desire to run away from home. I too tried to leave home one time, but it was a feeble effort. I sneaked through the woods to my friends home a half mile away without my mother's permission. She soon found me and convinced me that "I probably shouldn't ever, ever do that again," and I didn't.

There is a sense that tornadoes come, literally and figuratively, and blow us out of our Kansas. We get whacked, knocked and slapped around by events in traumatic ways. In his book, "Ruthless Trust," Brennan Manning describes it in these words: "When the shadow of Jesus' cross falls across our lives in the form of failure, rejection, abandonment, betrayal, unemployment, loneliness, depression, the loss of a loved one..."[xiii]

Who hasn't experienced one or more of these moments, felt emotions that come with it, and faced the spiritual struggle that follows? A deep friendship ends because of betrayal. Your regular income drops due to a downturn in the economy. Parents make empty promises to their children. In your time of need, everyone turns their back on you. Or, like Dorothy, you wake up to discover you aren't in Kansas anymore.

Reality hits hard—no soft padded gloves. We are shocked out of our comfort zone by the blast of an unexpected something. It takes away our security, and it feels like we have landed in a foreign country where all of the faces are different, rules have changed, and magic wizards control what takes place.

Yellow Brick Roads Have Detours

The Yellow Brick Road to our Oz doesn't go in a straight line. There are twists, turns and detours to be navigated. We can't draw a card that allows us to instantly bypass the angry apple trees, sleep producing poppies, or evil witches. You walk through them; not around them.

This shouldn't lead to fear, but should provide a test of the real world. This thing we call *life* isn't easy. There are trials, temptations and challenges at every corner. We can't fast forward past the bad parts so that we can camp out at the happy times. The only way to make it through is to admit our fears, face the challenge and keep moving forward. No quick fixes, instant answers or band-aid solutions will work.

Dorothy and her friends started their journey as frightened and uncertain individuals. They ended it with confidence, pride and determination. Real strength of character develops as we learn to persevere through the tough places. We face it. We take baby steps. Sometimes we can't take any steps at all. Standing up is all that we can do.

We turn onto the entrance to our "Highway to Happiness" and think all we need to do is keep it in the road and keep pushing the gas pedal. In an imaginary world, that might work. In ours, it won't. Life stories contains twists and turns we never imagined. Yet, it is in the delays and detours where we learn deep truths about ourselves and our purpose in being alive.

Even Our Best Supporters Have Missing Pieces

From the time Dorothy crashes in the land of the Munchkins, she begins a passionate journey to go back home again. Along the way she meets the Scarecrow, Tin Man and Lion. Each one needs one vital part to be complete. If the Scarecrow only had a brain, he could think like everyone else. If the Tin Man only had a heart, he could care and feel like others. If the Lion only had courage, he wouldn't live with fear. If Dorothy only had home, she wouldn't be wandering around in a dream trying to find her way back to Kansas.

Those who love and support us don't have to be perfect. In fact, they won't be completely whole. They have missing pieces. They don't always think clearly, feel deeply, act courageously and possess all the answers. Yet, they love us, and in that gift of love life opens up all its possibilities to us. Challenges can be faced together. Fear becomes a byproduct in dealing with evil forces. Courage moves us to state our needs and ask for help.

If this sounds a little like church, it should. I believe church was intended to be the place where we discover the brokenness of each other. We learn where some are strong and others are weak. We discover some of our pieces are missing, but that is okay. In His grace we learn all are loved, accepted, forgiven, healed and whole. We are a community of broken, caring people on a journey together. We discover the truth about ourselves, and we speak the truth to others. Why? Because somewhere in this world there needs to be people who love you enough to tell you who you are...broken, whole, sinner, forgiven, gifted, limited, loved and accepted.

I think we were created to live in community with one another. All of us are looking for The Yellow Brick Road and we all want others to help us look for it. Yet, in walking with others, we may discover it isn't in the color or direction of the road as much as it is in the gift of relationship.

I have come to believe that we have a family of birth and often this group provides all of our needs. For those who don't have that gift of family, they find it in a different way. Others may find the sense of family they need through friends with missing pieces. Either way, we find our home in this world with the people who become family to us.

Always Look Behind the Curtain

As the scarecrow described it, "Some people without brains do a whole lot of talking." Occasionally, these may come to us as wizards. To be a wizard means you practice magic or possess amazing skills and abilities. The Wizard of Oz supposedly possessed the ability to help people realize their dreams and find their missing pieces. In reality, he was just someone whose balloon sailed away and ended up in the Land of Oz.

It is interesting to note that wizards, whether real or imagined, do provide a good show. One will come along who states that he knows when the world will end, and followers line up to become believers. Another suggests that he has found the secret to financial success. All it takes is this course of CDs and $300 so that you can have a six-figure income while living on the beach. Someone else states they have the gift of healing, but it seems to be only given to a select few, not the needy masses.

Whether in Oz or in your life, please remember this thought: There is always someone or something standing behind the curtain pulling the levers, pushing buttons, creating smoke and shooting flames of fire. Another way to say it is, "Try to find out who or what is behind your curtain." It may be pain from the past or an unmet need, but some energy is making things take place.

Closely related to this thought is the fact that so often we rely on magical thinking. On the surface, we don't believe in magic wands, potions or spells. At a deeper level, we sometimes want people to instantly transport us out of our situation into a place of peace and happiness.

Own Your Journey

The most important lesson to me that comes from "The Wizard of Oz" is that you must own your journey. Your health, wellbeing and happiness do not depend upon witches, wizards, magic shoes, friends or even family. It doesn't depend upon what happened in the past, the threats that may loom over us, the magic forest around us... or singing "Somewhere over the Rainbow." It is your journey. You have been given a life. In it will come setbacks and success, pain and celebration, hurt and healing, and purpose and meaning. In relationship with God and those who love you, you put together the best life you can. You make choices and decisions. You question and listen. You hurt and heal. You find your way to the place that you never, ever want to leave again. It is your place, and no one can take it away from you.

There is a little bit of Oz in all of us. There are good and bad witches with which to contend, yellow brick roads to find and follow, wizards who pretend to have magical power and help us find the missing pieces, and "Somewhere Over the Rainbow" with wishes on stars.

With age, I think we come to realize that if we are going to find home in this world at all, we can't depend upon wizards in hot air balloons who don't know how to operate the equipment. We have to create it. We are born with family; we create family out of those individuals who come our way. It is a place. It is a feeling. It is a way of looking at our lives. It is waking up to the reality that we are created, gifted and called to be who we are. It is finding contentment in who we are, what has happened to us, and who we need to be as a person. We have learned to sit with our life and see in it all of the beauty of a divine plan lived by a very imperfect person and find in these moments a sense of peace.

Sacred Stories

"Will I Ever Get Over This?"

Three and a half years before my husband and I were married, we went through one of the most difficult experiences I have ever had to face. Before we started to date, Michael's mom was diagnosed with cancer and had fought it with everything she had for four years. On February 23, 2004, she lost her long-fought battle. After she had passed away, Michael felt like he needed to get away from everyone and find some space. He asked me to drive him around town so that he could process everything that had happened. We rode around the streets and country roads for hours that night. I will never forget how hard he cried and some of the words he said. We were stopped at a red light, and Michael turned to me and said, "Laura, this breaks my heart!" Tears streamed down my face. I didn't know what to say or how to react to this 19-year-old who talked like a little boy. He then asked me a question that I knew I didn't have the right answer to. He asked, "Will I ever get over this?"

I had no idea how to answer him, but I turned to him and said, "Yes!" I said, "Yes, you will move on from this one day. You will never forget your mom, you will never stop missing her, and you will always need her. But, yes, you will learn to move on from this."

With that answer, he looked at me and said, "OK, let's go back home". I'm not sure where that answer came from, but I knew it is what I needed to say. Every now and then, even six and a half years later, I still have to remind Michael that yes, everything will be OK. Yes, we miss her like crazy! Yes we wanted her at our wedding. Yes, we would give anything for her to meet our daughter. Yes, we think about her all of the time... But, yes, we will see her one day, and yes, she is always looking down on us.

    ~Laura Gregg Hardester

The Last Time We Talked

My name is Helen. My husband is Lonnie. We have been married 34 years and have five beautiful children. Lonnie had three daughters from his first marriage, and I had one daughter from mine. We had one son, Clint, together. Lonnie and I married when our children were all young, and they grew up to be a very close-knit group. Two of the girls live in Alabama, just across the river from Columbus, Ga. One is in Columbus, and the other one is in Fayetteville, Ga. We have 11 grandchildren. Clint, our baby and only son, lived in a town not too far from us. He dated his high school sweetheart for seven years. They were married in 2002, and in 2004 God blessed them with their first child, a son. Then in 2006, he blessed them with a second son. Life was good.

In March of 2009, Clint called and said we (as a whole family) didn't get together enough and wanted the whole group to take a trip. We have one grandson playing softball for a community college in Panama City, Fla., and he wanted us all to go watch him play baseball. It was really hard trying to get everyone's calendars together, but they made it work. They got on the Internet and started searching for a place to stay. They finally ended up with two two-bedroom condominiums in the same complex. We had a ball. We took pictures on the beach of the whole family and then each individual family together. We watched our grandson play baseball, and it was a great weekend.

Two weekends later, Clint died. I can't help but wonder if he somehow felt it was coming. In the three days before he passed, he came to see his dad and me every day. He was working, but he was the project manager for the company where he worked, and as long as everything was running smooth, he could come and go like he wanted. On Wednesday, he came and stayed a long time. He went down to the sandbar behind our house; his favorite place. He stayed most of the day then went back to work before going home to his wife and boys. On Thursday it was raining, so he picked his Dad up and they rode around all day. On Friday, his boss stopped by to visit with us for awhile. On Saturday, he and his wife attended a birthday party. They had a great time.

That evening, Clint and his wife were going to a wedding at Lake Blackshear, and he had asked me to keep the boys. I went to pick the boys up at the party, but it had not ended. I stayed a little while before we left. We stopped by the grocery store to pick up a few things, and the boys were so good. On the way home I called their daddy to tell him how good they were in the store. Little did I know that would be the last time I would ever speak to my baby boy.

They were headed to Lake Blackshear. His boss and family were headed to Florida on spring break, and he had given Clint the keys to his new corvette. He'd told him to have a good time at the wedding. Clint and his wife were at the reception after the wedding when Clint fell. I really don't know what time that was, but I'm guessing around 9:15 or 9:20. There were two off- duty EMTs at the reception. They started CPR as soon as he fell, but I'm told they never got a response.

Someone called us a few minutes later and asked, "What's going on with Clint?" We didn't know anything, but learned that he had fallen at the reception and was taken by ambulance to a nearby hospital. Then we began to receive non-stop calls. It was hectic to say the least. We put the boys in the car and hurried to the hospital.

Everything was a complete blur. I remember family, friends and church members gathering. We sat...we waited...we wondered what was taking place. Around 10:30 the doctor opened the door to where we all were waiting and simply said, "I'm sorry. We did all we could do."

That's when my world as I had known it ended. All of our lives changed that night. We had to call our other children. I barely remember any of it. It's just a fog. I know I wouldn't leave the hospital. I had to see my baby. It had to be a mistake...but it wasn't.

I do remember all the family and church members that came to the hospital that night. It was amazing; so many people, so much love and support. I guess that's how we made it through the next few days. Clint's wife was in a daze. We all were, but she had lost her husband and her boys' father. Our daughters had lost their brother. Lonnie and I had lost our baby, our only son.

Parents are not supposed to outlive their children. I think that is the worst pain that you can live through on this earth. A part of us that we will never get back is gone. Everybody is trying to get on with their lives. It's been a year and a half, and it has not gotten any easier.

I need to add that Clint died with Fatal Arrhythmia. This means his heart went out of rhythm, and they couldn't get it back. On the Wednesday before he passed, he had a full physical with an EKG for an upcoming job they were starting, and he passed it with flying colors. They told him he was in great shape, and he looked like the perfect picture of health.

All this tells me is that it was meant to be. It was God's plan. Clint never smoked a cigarette, never did a drug, and would only occasionally have a drink. It was just God's plan. He had led several people to Christ and was talking to several more. He touched so many lives. He was ours, but he was a really good man. For whatever reason God put him on this earth, he had completed it. It was his time to go home.

I don't know— I'm still in denial. It's like I can't let my heart know what my mind knows. I know that sounds crazy but it's where I am right now. Lonnie and I go to the cemetery almost every day. I feel nothing, because I've blocked it. I can't stand the pain, and my mind knows that.

He was my baby, and yes, I was mad with God at one time, but I've gotten past that hurdle. Lonnie says he feels closer to God now than he did before we lost Clint. I don't know that I've gotten there yet. Pretty sure I haven't. I do know with all my heart that Clint is in heaven. He was a good man, a good husband, and fantastic father and son, and I know I have to live my life so that I will see him again when the time comes.

Right now I pretty much live day by day. So I guess that answers how I live YES in a NO world. It's so I can see my son again one day. That's not the only reason, of course, but the biggest one at this moment. I guess it will get better with time. When you lose a child you lose a part of you that you'll never get back. I've always been funny—cut up, laughed, joked, enjoyed life—but right now my funny is gone. I lost my funny when I lost my Clint, and I can't find it.

I thank God every day for those two beautiful grandsons he left us. I go down to the sandbar behind the house almost every day. It was Clint's favorite place, and I can understand why. It is so peaceful and beautiful down there.

~**Helen Peaster**

A Different Kind of Christmas

Christmas 2009 was not our normal holiday. Our youngest daughter, Courtney, was pregnant with her third baby, and her due date was Christmas day. Since her first two, both girls, were born after their due date, we thought this might happen again. When her doctor's visit confirmed it would be a few more days, we bundled up her two girls, then four and 15 months, and brought them home with us to spend a few days.

My husband, Rick, is the play-by-play announcer for a college men's basketball team, and he was scheduled to leave for a trip to North Carolina on December 28. When he left for his trip, I took the girls to our oldest daughter, Allison's, for an overnight visit. We went back to our house the next day so we could pack and get them back to their home in Birmingham on the 30th.

After dinner and their baths, we played for awhile, and they both fell asleep, the 15-month-old in my lap. After she was sound asleep, I stood up from the sofa with her in my arms to carry her to her bed. As I did, I stepped down on a toy with wheels, and it began to roll. My left foot started rolling and my right foot got caught under the sofa, and I went nowhere! As I was falling, I

172

looked back and could see my guardian angel helping me to the floor. I fell straight down on my knee before landing on my back. The baby never woke up.

When I realized what had happened, I struggled to get to my feet and knew then something was wrong. I could not put any weight on my right leg. I dragged my leg and the baby up the stairs to put her in bed. I came back down the stairs by bouncing on my bottom, got to the phone and called Allison. "I've taken a fall, hurt my leg, and think I need to go to the ER." She and her husband, Scott, took their children to his mother's house and made the hour drive to come help me. She and I went to the hospital. The X-rays revealed a fracture. They gave me a shot and a leg brace and told me I needed to see an orthopedic surgeon.

Thankfully, my job with a college athletic department gave access to an athletic trainer who was able to get me in to see the surgeon the next morning. I knew I was in trouble when he walked in the examining room after having seen the X-ray's and said, "How in the h#&& did you break your knee? Nobody ever breaks their knee!" I was sent home with instructions to not even put my toe on the floor, a brace that would not let me bend my leg, and a bottle of pain killers.

My wonderful sister and brother-in-law basically moved in with us for the New Year's weekend. They cooked, we cried, ate, watched football, played cards and cried some more. I had several pity parties over the next few weeks.

On January 5, I was scheduled for surgery, ironically, at the same time Courtney was being induced into labor to deliver a baby that was 11 days late. I was devastated that we could not be there with her.

Once again, my wonderful family came to the rescue. My brother-in-law, Randy, and his daughter, Lindsay, drove to Birmingham with a movie camera to capture the birth of our fifth grandchild. They started recording in the parking lot and recorded the whole day for us. Every moment was saved and put to music. We were able to experience every moment as though we were there. This was definitely a YES in a NO world. Neither of us realized what a special gift we had been given. We were both in tears as we watched it over and over again.

When I came out of surgery, Allison and Rick assured me the birth of our grandson in Birmingham was going well, and we should have a baby soon. However, I knew something was not exactly right, there were a lot of secret phone calls being made around me, and no one wanted to give me direct answers to my questions.

After a time in the recovery room, I was allowed to go home. Armed with several prescriptions, a morphine pump, and a bandage from my ankle to my hip, Allison and Rick loaded me up and took me home. At home I settled into bed and took some medication for pain before drifting off to sleep. It wasn't long before I was awakened by the doorbell ringing. I wasn't completely surprised since we had so many family and friends stopping by for visits with food or cards. I looked up to see my boss of 13 years at the door and soon learned he had not only come to check on me but also to drop another big NO in my life— he would no longer be in his position. Now, I understood why there were so many calls in the background during my surgery and recovery. I held one of the most enjoyable jobs of my life, and he was such a big part of that. Now I didn't know what his absence would mean to my future. He left, and I drifted back to sleep hoping that when I woke up all of this would have been a dream, but it wasn't.

I moved through the next few days in a fog. I was depressed that I couldn't be with Courtney and the baby, I couldn't even put my toes on the floor, and my world at work was going to change. There were a lot of NO's in my life at this point. I have to admit, my faith wavered at times—there were some very dark moments. I hoped that this was it and that things would start to look up soon.

Courtney was dismissed from the hospital but without the baby who had developed pneumonia and was moved to the Neonatal Intensive Care Unit. I know the Lord doesn't put more on us than we can handle, but at that point I had reached my limit! I wasn't sure I could handle any more setbacks.

After 12 days in the NICU, our new grandson, Conner, went home from the hospital. Thankfully, my mom was able to spend time with Courtney and take care of the girls so she could go to the hospital. In February, Courtney was finally able to travel out of town with the baby, so she brought him to see us for the first time. It was a month after his birth, but YES, he was beautiful and healthy! Tears filled our eyes and joy flooded our hearts as we held him for the first time.

Rick continued to travel with his job, so Allison and her children came to the house after school to help me get a shower and eat. They would spend the night and head back to school the next morning. My sister, Dianne, took vacation days to spend with me—I can't imagine where I would have been without my family. I will never be able to thank them enough.

When I returned to work, I was in a wheelchair. I started rehabilitation, so Rick took me to work, came back and took me to rehab, went back to work and then picked me up in the afternoon. He was such a trooper! During this time, he started having trouble with his knee. Our doctor did an MRI and discovered a torn MCL. The doctor wouldn't do surgery until I was mobile enough to take care of Rick. In April, Rick had his surgery.

At last we were both back on our feet, and things were starting to get back to normal—or so we thought. I had transitioned into my new work situation when the doctor discovered the screw placed in my knee had developed an infection around it. He said it needed to stay in at least a year for the healing process to be complete, but we had to monitor it. He ordered another X-ray and confirmed the need for surgery to replace the original hardware. After 12 months, two surgeries, weeks of rehabilitation, a wheelchair, walker, crutches, cane, the doctor released me. On top of that was my husband's surgery and birth of a grandchild. It was an eventful year and certainly not the Christmas we expected.

YES, we were ready to put 2010 behind us and not look back. My faith never let me down, even though there were dark times when I began to wonder. God is so good and He has blessed us tremendously. I know there are people in much worse situations, but after having several NO's thrown at us, I feel we came out much stronger, and our YES has made our lives even more meaningful!

~*Myra Cameron*

In a Time of Need

I'd like to share some personal experiences with you. These have enabled me to see God use everyday people to be priests to me during some very difficult times in my life. Out of these trials has come a desire for me to share God's love with others. My *prayer is that by saying YES to this writing experience, I'll be able to make a difference in the lives of others.*

In January of 1992, my husband and I were awakened early one morning by a phone call from a relative. There had been a house fire at the home where my Mom and Dad were visiting. Three people did not survive. My father, a 15-year-old granddaughter of my aunt, and a handicapped child from the center where my aunt worked were killed in the fire. My mother had sustained second and third degree burns on 40 to 45 percent of her body. Most all of her burns were upper body ones except for her feet, and she had breathed smoke and flames directly into her lungs causing them to be severely damaged. She was admitted into a Burn Intensive Care Unit in Florida.

Before we could do anything, our home was flooded with people. I could not begin to list the names of all of those who came to support, but YES, I still remember the love on each face. These included relatives, friends, neighbors, church family and work associates. Don't ever use the excuse, "I don't know what to do or say." Your presence is an act of love that will never be forgotten.

As I think back to that early morning phone call, those first few hours were very painful! I was a daddy's girl. My Daddy was gone, and I didn't get to see him or tell him goodbye! I remember thinking that this could not be happening to my family again. One month prior to the fire, I lost my grandmother to a stroke. Pain from the past has a way of resurfacing when you experience loss again. Three years prior to the fire, friends pulled into my driveway to break the news of a tragic automobile accident that had claimed the life of my baby brother who was only 23 at the time. Feeling this hurt again, I began to wonder... I recall thinking, "Father, I'm sinking. I cannot accept this! I did not get to tell my brother goodbye. I didn't get to tell my daddy goodbye. Where are you in the midst of all this? I need you! Father, this is too much, too quick! I can't accept it!"

During the hours of shock over the loss of Daddy, we stayed in constant communication with the hospital. We were advised to get there as quickly as possible if we wanted Mother to recognize us. In a daze, I realized plans had to be made, but words cannot express the helplessness I felt. I knew that we had a funeral to plan for my father, but at the same time my mother was in critical condition 12 hours away from our home. As I look back over this tragedy, YES, I can thank God for those who ministered to my family and me.

Our next-door neighbor, who had been Mom and Dad's pastor, spent the night with us holding us up in prayer. Our pastor was there to be with my husband as he broke the news to his mother and father. My husband's sister and her husband came to be with us. She took charge of making and receiving phone calls. My sister-in-law arranged for the pilot of a private plane to fly my only sister, two brothers, and me to Florida to be with my mom. My husband's father and mother took care of the financial arrangements. I can still see the faces of our loved ones as the plane took off with us. Our hurt was shared by so many! We received the call at 1:30 a.m., and by 3 p.m. that same day we landed and headed to the hospital.

When I walked into my mother's hospital room, I wasn't prepared to see her in this condition. Due to the amount of burns she had suffered, she was swollen beyond recognition. She couldn't see, she couldn't speak, but we sensed that somehow she knew we were there.

Things began to happen so fast. We were bombarded with medical questions and decisions. We were approached with questions about a living will. My brothers, sister and I talked about it but could not reach an agreement. We were still in shock over the loss of our Father. Now we were being approached with the "what ifs" concerning our mother. This was only the beginning of seeing answered prayers. The social worker said Mom wasn't capable of making a decision, and it was unfair for us. So, we waited, not knowing what we were waiting for.

I felt the weight of the world on my shoulders. The morning had been very hectic. It included meeting with Mom's doctor. We were advised that skin graft surgery must begin as quickly as possible in an effort to reduce the risk of infection. I interpreted this to mean that it would need to take place before we returned home to make funeral arrangements for Dad. We were also introduced to the nursing staff. We learned they worked 7 days on and 7 days off. We struggled with leaving Mother to undergo surgery while leaving her in the hands of nurses that we had not had time to meet.

With my heart so heavy, I found my way to the little hospital chapel that morning. I did not feel that I could not go on. How I needed strength and comfort! I knelt to pray. When I arose from the kneeling position, I felt a gentle touch on my shoulder. I turned and looked into the most beautiful caring eyes that I had ever seen. The words that came from this young lady were so gentle and kind. "You look like you're hurting so bad," she said. YES! I was able to spill out all of the hurt, pain, and losses that I had tried to hold inside in an effort to remain in control. God knew I needed that priest that morning. Our paths may never cross again, but how I thanked God for sending her to me to just listen and share my grief. I still recall stroking her golden blonde hair to convince myself that she was real and not an angel. She was so beautiful and had such a gentle spirit! I later learned she was a college student who came by the chapel every morning to begin her day in prayer.

On one occasion while sitting in the waiting room, I was called to the phone. A voice I had never heard before introduced himself as a nephew to someone who lived in our small town. He had heard about the tragedy on the news. He introduced his mother to me over the phone. This brief introduction was the beginning of a lasting relationship. This dear lady had us in her home many times during Mother's hospitalization for a night's sleep, a hot meal and companionship. It was the closest thing to a home away from home for me. YES, God's timing is perfect! We had been in the home of this kind lady for a short while when we learned that she had lost her husband to cancer a few short months prior to our crisis.

My brother and I sat in the waiting room one night so lonely, tired and desperately needing a touch from God to confirm His love for us. The phone rang. The lady on the other end introduced herself to us. She told us she had heard of the tragedy through a friend. She had prayers over the phone with us. Later, she sat with us through a long night of waiting and praying when we were told that Mother would not make it through the night. This little lady told her pastor about us. It was not long before the entire congregation was lifting us in prayer.

I'll never forget the time I hung the phone up from talking to my husband and our son (who at that time was only 9 years old). The tears were still streaming down my cheeks. I was so homesick. I got up and looked around. There stood the pastor from this little lady's church.

The funds were low because we had been there almost a month straight. Mother was still too critical for us to leave or to be transported closer to home. We were so homesick! The pastor turned and shook my hand. He said he hoped that we would understand. He handed us a card with a check in it. YES! God's "priesthood of all believers" in a church unfamiliar to us had seen a need and responded.

My mother remained at this burn unit from January 31 until May 25. She was placed on a ventilator and was given less than a 5 percent chance to live when she first arrived. During her stay she underwent seven skin graft surgeries, and she became septic throughout her body causing her to gain over 100 lbs of fluid weight. Complications caused her to lose over half of both feet. Mother was in the hospital for more than six months, on a ventilator for 115 days, and on a trachea for 45 of those days. But through it all, we were learning to put our trust in God.

I cannot sit here typing this out and pretend that these tragedies in my life have not been painful. But YES, I can rejoice and give God the praise for seeing miraculous healing take place in Mom's life. We still don't have all the answers to so many questions. I still have to wonder why Dad's life was taken the way that it was. But through God's grace we are making it "One Day at a Time." We have learned to change the questions from "Why" to "How." How can this that has happened in our life bring glory to God? How can we take what has happened to us and use it to be there for someone else who's hurting?

God has opened many doors for us to share these experiences with others. Mother and I have shared in several churches and groups both in our hometown and out of town. Even though this can be painful...I stand amazed at the "sense of humor" that Mother has. This little lady was a quiet little woman who would never have dreamed of getting up in front of a group. But we realized that God was not finished with this little lady yet. When

she stands (and notice that I said stands) before a group (even though she's left with less than half of both feet) God speaks through her. She shares how God was "working things out" before this accident. She shares what a blessing she gets singing and praising God, but I know that God is still using her to continue to touch the lives of others.
   ~Willa Dean Gregg

When YES Turned To NO

We were happily married for two years when God blessed us with our daughter, Sarah. Around two years later we decided it was time to increase the family yet again. Two days after Sarah's second birthday, we found out that I was expecting. Our prayers were answered, "Yes, you may have another precious one of mine." We were so excited. We shared the news with family, friends and complete strangers.
   The day of the first ultrasound came, and we went to see our little dot of love on the screen. Everything looked fine; however measurements indicated he was not as far along as we thought he should be. The doctor said to come back in two weeks. We waited.
   The day before our appointment, I realized I had not been nauseated in quite some time. Concern turned to fear. We went to the appointment on Thursday. Our lives changed. Our child no longer had a heart beat. He had not grown. Though his body was with me, God was holding our son. By that afternoon the miscarriage had begun. Tearfully we went to the hospital the next morning. August 1, 2008 we said goodbye, for now, to our son.

Why did God say yes? Why had God allowed us to become pregnant only to take away our child? These are questions I have stopped asking, but it took time. I don't know why God said yes, but He did. He allowed us to have our son for a short while. For this we are thankful.

How could we continue to show our faith through this? It was hard. We knew God had a purpose but it did not take away the hurt. We prayed and were prayed for. Could we continue on with our daily lives while suffering, while in pain? YES, we were able to show that Christ is in all things, and that we trust in Him. God has a plan.

For I know the plans I have for you," declares the Lord, "plans to prosper you and not to harm you, plans to give you hope and a future. (Jeremiah 29:11)

To date we have shared with three other couples who have been through the same loss of a child. Through the pain we have experienced, we are able to witness, comfort and guide others to where hope and love abound. We are able to share with them that, YES; life will get easier, with time, and the gentle touch of God's hand. Six months after losing our son, we were surprised to learn that God had blessed us once again. Our second daughter, Leah, was born a year and 20 days after the loss of our son. We would not have Leah now if God had not taken our son to live with Him. We continue to find comfort knowing that one day our entire family will be together, in God's Kingdom.

~Abby Miller Martin

Reflections

I believe that the Creator of the universe granted freedom to everything that exists. It was built into the blueprint of life. This grants people the opportunity to make choices and exercise their power in the course or direction of what takes place in their world. This same freedom was granted for all creation "according to its kind." Each facet of existence was blessed with freedom and power to pursue its purpose.

In this design of freedom, life becomes more unpredictable and random. The divine creator isn't located on a celestial cloud pushing buttons and watching people squirm or jump.

So where is he? For me the answer is in Christ. The Gospel of John reads, "In the beginning was the Word, and the Word was with God, and the Word was God." God became incarnate in Christ that we might understand his true nature. It is the desire to be with us. It is a place. It is a relationship. It is companionship through the adversity.

Adversity happens because life happens. It takes place according to the laws of nature. So, what do I do with adversity? It becomes a companion to my experience. It becomes my teacher. I ask it questions. I listen. I walk into it. I listen to what is being said about me and my existence. I pay attention. I allow it to help me learn deeper truths. I let the pain flow over, around and through me. I let it carry me to a new place; a different place than where I started. I allow it to help me let go of the superficial and search for permanent truths. I become a student of my own loss, grief and struggle. I ask God to walk with me, stand with me, give me strength, help me hurt, hold me in his arms of Grace, accept me as a broken person, let his strength shine through my limitations, and give me the opportunity for a second, third or fourth chance to start over again. For I live, as one store suggests, in "The Do-Over Place" all of the time.

Healing Souls

A Prayer for Healing Souls

Heavenly Father,

We cannot heal ourselves. We do not have the solution. We have joined every "instant answer, automatic solution, and magical word club" we can find all to no avail.

Our lives are broken. The pieces lie all around us on the floor. Take our brokenness, we pray, and work your grace into our hearts and souls. We are restless. We want answers. We want them now.

Help us to hear—"you are my child—in you I am well pleased."

Help us to release control of our lives. May we surrender to the warm embrace of your gracious love. Help us to trust you even when we cannot see the way. Help us to walk forward as you, the gentle Shepherd, lead us into new pastures of nourishment and renewal.

*Thank you, O' God, for the gift of **another** beginning.*

In Christ's Name,

Amen

Creating a Second Journey

The night before my father died, I had stayed with one of my uncles and his family in town. Early the next morning another uncle came to pick me up and take me home. I was expecting to go to the hospital because that was my daily routine. When we arrived at our house in the country, he drove up the gravel drive and pulled into the yard. I was surprised to see so many cars. We had not had visitors in months. I walked into the living room to find my mother sitting in a chair while family and friends stood around her. She hugged me as she cried.

My brother, Robert, immediately suggested, "Randy let's go round up the pigs." Sounds like an odd thing to say, but back then we raised a few in a pen near our barn. Some had dug a hole under the fence and were eating corn in the field in front of the house. At the age of 20, he either was asked or volunteered to break the news to me that our dad had died. As we moved the pigs back toward the barn, he began, "Randy, you know how Daddy has been very sick lately. Well, he died this morning." I started to cry and he responded with, "Now, you are going to have to stop crying because that will just get Mom more upset."

I believe that is the only time anyone ever engaged with me about the experience of losing my dad—the day a 20-year-old young man was given or accepted the task of telling his 9-year-old little brother the most difficult news of all. Life really isn't fair. Little boys aren't supposed to lose their parents.

Twenty-year-olds aren't supposed to be the messengers of life's traumas. You don't share tough messages while chasing pigs. You don't stifle your emotions so others will have an easier experience. You don't bottle up your pain and not talk about it.

In some ways, I emotionally lingered in the field chasing pigs, because no one ever helped me go back home again, and I wasn't old enough or smart enough to know how to do it myself. Why? I don't know all of the reasons. Now, it doesn't matter, because that is an image that is pretty powerful for me. I think it represents the way, even today, that we all process our setbacks, adversity and difficulties. It comes unexpectedly. Our routine changes. We pretend to be strong so others won't be bothered. The pain lingers beneath the surface pulling the strings of our emotional world like a puppeteer might guide a puppet to hop and jump. We chase pigs out in front of the house or perform some other normal activity until we find a way to create another sense of home with different people in a different place.

According to my friend Carol Mathias, "Woundedness creates the journey." When my dad died, my journey changed. I didn't know it, nor could I realize how dramatically my destination had just been altered. All of this was taking place without my permission. I healed some. There was a funeral. I cried, my brother and mother cried. We struggled with the sudden sense of loss. There was a service, a grave and a marker. There were flowers. Friends and family gathered. People shook our hands. Some held us in long embraces.

We went back home. But home had changed. There was an empty spot. There was a void of personality. There was a large presence of compassion missing.

I didn't heal completely. I didn't get to say goodbye. I didn't talk through my emotions with anyone. There wasn't a person or relationship that allowed a little boy to describe how his world had changed or how much he hurt because the one he dearly loved had suddenly left. The pain became permanent. Like a squatter taking up residence in a vacant house, pain moved into my heart. It never left. In fact, it traveled with me everywhere I went.

There came a time when I began to take steps toward healing the hurt that had begun so many years ago. One spring I grew weary of telling the story over and over the same way. I tired of facing the same struggles of the spirit. This need for change had been present for quite some time. I found a journal where I had attempted to record my thoughts and reflections. In reading notes from years past, I found that I written the same words for three straight years.

Guy Sayles, a friend, shares a very clear and powerful observation about age that I think holds value for my own journey. In a note he penned for a social media site, he observes:

> *"There comes a point in life where the statute of limitations runs out on blaming other people for what our lives have become. Mature adults don't keep protesting against the distant past and drawing up indictments against people who, long ago, failed them, hurt them, or disappointed them in some way. When it becomes clear that we can't shift blame any more to "them"—to parents or teacher or bosses or spouses or children or God—then we are in midlife.xiv"*

191

Maybe some of my struggle has been the loss of loved ones, unrealistic expectations I have created for myself, or possibly the aging process altogether. There is an old saying that suggests: "When the student is ready, the teacher will appear." That day arrived for me. Through the skilled coaching of a friend who happens to be a therapist and colleague, I was able to see that "all of our past is preparation for who we are now." This insight opened up a door to a new purpose, passion and power. The world of pain and faith became integrated. I could see where you constantly hold life in tension; there is joy and sadness; there is pain and healing; there is doubt and trust; there is hope and uncertainty handcuffed together with our own trust and resistance.

Over a period of time, I unpacked old hurt. I cleaned out memory closets and threw away outdated ways of looking at life. I read scripture through new eyes. I could see that Jesus Christ was not only God with us, he was also a model for living authentically. His words revealed the nature of God but also communicated truth for everyday life. He lived YES in a NO world and never wavered, stopped or turned aside. He challenged individuals and asked, "Do you want to be healed?" (John 5:6)

I had preached sermons about Jesus for many years. There came a time when I let him do more than just "save" me—I allowed him to heal me. I gave him permission to walk down the hallways of my memory, and as he did, he became the tour guide and I became the tourist in my own life. I wanted to ask him, "Why did this event or that experience take place?" He helped me see those were not relevant questions to a meaningful life. He began to speak to me through scripture but also through the words of others. New faces and new voices began to knock on my door. Those I needed found me rather than me finding them. Then I realized a new truth. He had always been with me. The unseen presence in every life experience—he was there. My life wasn't just a series of broken dreams, but it was a beautiful stained glass window created from pieces welded together by His divine love. And then I knew—I was one of God's sacred gifts to the world. I was a gift of love to someone.

I do not want to suggest that I have found the answer to life's great questions. Instead, I only want to share what I have learned on my journey. As we walk along the pathway that we think will lead us to success, happiness or peace, life happens. It hits us hard; it knocks us off of the road we thought we would travel. We hurt. Our spirits become wounded. It is in the brokenness that we find healing. Our wounds create the journey to an "adjusted destination." If we hear this deep within, then we realize we must recreate ourselves with new people, destination and purpose. If we don't hear it, we wander around aimlessly, trying to live our lives with someone else's values rather than our own. We live with used words—inherited, borrowed—but never ones we have voiced from the deep places in our own being.

It was through this insight that I realized the past and present were pieces of the same puzzle. I didn't arrive at the destination I thought I would reach, but I wasn't supposed to. My place in this world is different and it needs to be. I have lived a wonderful life. It is God's gift to me, and I am one of his many, many gifts to the world. In that thought, there is contentment and peace. I live from a different place.

I have come to embrace an intentional life. I walk to the beat of a different drum. I am nontraditional. I don't fit the mold, norm or expectation of being a minister or even a person, and I don't want to. I am called to be someone else; I am called to be me. If I live that call with any sense of courage and effort, that is enough. It is all I am supposed to do.

Other Lessons

There are some other lessons that have been discovered over the years. These are ones that I have harvested from a long journey of reflecting on my life.

- If we don't address our pain and hurts, we end up chasing pigs in the fields of our lives for a long, long time.
- Unprocessed pain continues to haunt us and hold us back even though we desire to move forward.
- Well-meaning loved ones may not be able to help us because they have their own stuff to process.
- Holding our hurt inside for the sake of others or appearances is not an effective solution.
- Trying to be strong to maintain an image of strength is a waste of time and energy. Strong people are the ones who own their wounds and let them become sources of grace.
- No one can heal for us; we must put our own junk on the table.
- Woundedness creates a different path than the one we expected to follow.
- Adversity requires us to do some soul work to heal our broken spirits.

Maybe this is why we spend more energy avoiding, denying and pretending adversity doesn't exist. It requires a lot of courage and effort to work your way through the tough places of life.

Hidden Landmarks

Silent Influences

I stayed with a great aunt and uncle a lot while my father was in the hospital. They were a delightful retired couple who had no children of their own, but they were gracious and loving to me. The routine was the same every day.

I'd arrive in time to eat breakfast and work in the garden or yard until lunch. After eating a freshly cooked meal and a brief rest, Aunt Maddie would take me fishing at a small river behind her home.

Walking across the field until we came to the trees, we would locate a small path that would lead down a sloping hill to the river. The place where we fished had a landmark—a large boulder about the size of a small car rested in the middle of the stream. Slow-moving water flowed easily around the smooth sides of this large rock. Since it didn't rise very far out of the water, it would often become covered when the river flooded. Even when the water would rise, you could see where the boulder changed the course of the river though it was hidden beneath the surface.

This single childhood memory has served as a reminder for me of an important truth. We all have landmarks hidden beneath the surface that direct the currents of our lives. They cannot be seen. Their influence is consistent in every word and action. Like giant boulders settled on the bottom of the river bed, they force the currents of energy, relationships and decisions to move around their space and find another direction. We may believe we are making conscious, intentional choices, but we aren't capable. Why? We can't move the rocks. They are permanently fixed; anchored in the sands of our time.

I was in Savannah, Ga., for work, and early one morning I was driving a few blocks from the hotel to the client's office. A large delivery truck stopped right in front of me. The driver stepped down out of the cab and marched into a restaurant. An employee from the restaurant walked out to my window and delivered a brief message, "He's stopped—you will need to go around."

At first I was a little irritated—OK, a lot. Then a thought occurred. I want to be like that big truck. Sometimes I want to stop life and tell everyone else, "You will need to go around me."

It doesn't work that way. Life comes at, through, and over but doesn't often go around. Instead, it leaves tread marks on us where it didn't stop but kept right on rolling over who we are and what we wanted to take place. Our friends planned a spring, outdoor wedding for their daughter. It was in a quiet setting surrounded by restored homes and beautifully landscaped gardens. Everything was set up outside. First, the clouds came. Then the rain arrived. It didn't just rain; there was a deluge. A tent was rented. No relief in sight. It rained so hard that the groomsmen and bridesmaids walked from the building to the tent under large golf umbrellas. Life didn't stop for a wedding.

Life leaves landmarks. Like a boulder in the middle of the stream, death leaves loss and grief. Divorce leaves doubt and confusion. Abuse leaves hurt and betrayal. Unless you deal with it or work through it, this large "boulder of life experience," lingers under the emotional surface diverting the currents in a different direction than you would want. That thought creates fear for many people—the reality that there are questions or uncertainties that they are not ready to face. Life can't be fixed, but it can be lived. Fear becomes the critical emotion. The more you dwell on the obstacle, the larger it grows, eventually to the point that it paralyzes a person.

Deep End of the Pool

I was fortunate to have a very supportive extended family. Bud and Alice Gregg were not only my uncle and aunt they were our neighbors as well. Aunt Alice included me when her children began swimming lessons in the summer. As a child, I played around and in the water but had not learned to swim. I was afraid. I didn't want to relax or surrender to someone else's direction. Someone would try to hold me to float, but I couldn't just rest in their arms. I was terrified.

In desperation, my swimming instructor took me to the deep end of the pool. The water was at least eight feet deep. I stood on the edge. She entered the water where she invited, encouraged, pleaded, threatened, and used any other motivational technique she could imagine. Finally, she told me, "I will catch you." There was something about her offer that finally struck a nerve. I think her influence was strengthened by the fact that she was 18, and very pretty, and I was 10 or 11 and didn't want to appear to be childish and unable to do this simple task. So I jumped. I came up instinctively dog paddling, and she caught me. Fear left instantly. I had done something that I had never imagined. I began to jump over and over again all over the place. At first there was a little hesitation, but that soon evolved into bold confidence.

In many ways we avoid swimming in the deep end of the pool and stay paralyzed on the side of life. We walk up to the edge, and we want to jump into the deep water, but we don't. Then we walk away beating ourselves up for being afraid, one more time. Fear is a wonderful emotion. It causes us to be alert and pay attention to uncertain situations. It causes us to run away from harm. When it operates as designed, fear becomes the protector from all that might bring hurt or injury to us.

As a part of our genetic code, fear was bestowed to protect us from danger. Our ancestors centuries ago instantly knew to run from wild animals, flee falling rocks, or avoid wildfires. Fear was the original "911 emotional signal" designed to protect us from harm. Due to influences from parents and significant people in our lives, we train our original "fear factor" to be on alert for anything we perceive to be dangerous. Unfortunately, this redefinition moves from animals, people or events that are truly dangerous to those that are imagined to be dangerous. In our new vocabulary, it becomes a very scary thing to face anything threatening. We face a new situation— the unknown—we hit the fear button and the signal comes through—"Be afraid; be very afraid." And what happens? We become terrified.

What does this have to do with healing your life? To be honest, it has everything to do with it. Until you face your fears and stare into the eyes of what you dread most, you aren't likely to heal. You will spend more energy avoiding, explaining, or making excuses than you will finding a path toward being whole.

Kidnapped as an 11-year-old, Jaycee Dugard was held captive for 18 years in a compound in her captor's backyard. According to news accounts, her physical space consisted of a series of sheds, tents and tarpaulins. She was found and released in 2009. In an interview with Diane Sawyer that aired on ABC, Jaycee stated, "Why not look at it? Stare it down until it can't scare you anymore. I don't want there to be any more secrets."xv

I am deeply impressed with this young lady's strength of character and courage to make a new start after alleged abuse for so many years. Her words, "Stare it down until it can't scare you anymore," offer a powerful example for anyone who has been surprised by life. You have to look into the face of fear. You have to look into the eyes of that which you dread the most. You have to "stare it down." Until you do, you will live in whatever arrangements fear dictates. It will be some state of constant upheaval, uncertainty and doubt. Your YES for life will be only the one that fear allows you to have, not the one you were created to live. Your existence will be rooted in the past, what might have been, or where your fantasy takes you, but it will not be real, authentic or owned by you.

For this reason, I think you have to look beneath the surface and find the landmarks that are diverting the current. Look at what they are. Go back to where they began. Pick them apart. Find out what you lost but also what you gained from the experience. Learn to see them for what they are—landmarks of life. These will be places where your life changed but not one where you have to permanently reside. These are simply turning points for a new beginning.

Receiving and Letting Go

There is a constant movement of life. You feel the flow of inhaling breath and the outward flow of exhaling breath. This incoming and outgoing, holding and releasing, occurs in each moment and relationship. It reflects the tension and dynamics we must balance—knowing when to hold and when to release. This isn't an experience new to our generation. The writer of the Book of Ecclesiastes in chapter 3 states:

> [1] There is a time for everything,
> and a season for every activity under the heavens:
> [2] a time to be born and a time to die,
> a time to plant and a time to uproot,
> [3] a time to kill and a time to heal,
> a time to tear down and a time to build,
> [4] a time to weep and a time to laugh,
> a time to mourn and a time to dance,
> [5] a time to scatter stones and a time to gather them,
> a time to embrace and a time to refrain from embracing,
> [6] a time to search and a time to give up,
> a time to keep and a time to throw away,
> [7] a time to tear and a time to mend,
> a time to be silent and a time to speak,
> [8] a time to love and a time to hate,
> a time for war and a time for peace.
> (Ecclesiastes 3).

Coming and Going

Life comes and life goes. Each day offers the privilege to be alive—we breathe, move, experience, and spend time doing the things we enjoy. Life goes. These moments do not last forever. They move swiftly by like the current in a fast-moving stream. Here for a second; moving in another direction in the next moment.

Birthdays come and birthdays go.

People enter our lives; people leave our lives.

One day begins; another day ends.

A new idea emerges; an old one exits.

A new expectation forms; an old expectation draws to a close.

If we can receive life as it comes to us and enjoy the moments of the gift, then we can appreciate the coming as well as the going. Life moves by us. Life moves in us. We move with life. We receive it; we release it. A continuous flow of moments passes around us; we embrace; we let go; and life moves forward.

We receive it as a gift to be unwrapped and opened. We embrace the moment, fully present to the pleasure and the pain, letting life teach us what we need to know.

If we cannot receive the events and people in our lives, then we resist and fail to receive them. We want them to be different. So, we take steps to control—on our terms. We stand still. We stop. We dream of what might have been. We complain. We whine. We expect a different set of circumstances or relationships to develop.

Grasping and Holding

Unfortunately, we want to own life. We want it to stand still in the form or in the way we want it to be. We spend our energy trying to own things. We work to own a job that will offer income and security. We want to own relationships that will provide intimacy and connection. We want to own outcomes, whether that is a dream, a state of being, or a plan of action. The thought seems to be that if we can own it, we can control it—or so we lead ourselves to believe. We enter conversations believing that we can control the outcome. In fact, we focus so much energy on the end result that we lose sight of the privilege or pleasure of being in the discussion.

This desire to grasp and hold reflects an egotistical need to control. We want things to go our way. If we are honest, we want relationships that meet our needs, conversations that satisfy our emotional desire to connect, or encouragement that provides the support we hunger to find. Holding and grasping gives us a false sense of security. So, we want to hold and grasp. We want it in our hands. We grip it tightly as though we can control it by holding it more tightly. But we can't. The more we try to dictate outcomes the less influence we actually have. We focus more of our thoughts and energy on trying to direct or guide someone or something toward our goal that we lose the opportunity to embrace or enjoy the moments being shared.

There is a season for learning to let go. Pain serves a healthy purpose. It reminds us of loss and grief. Yet, if we hold onto the pain, it lingers way beyond the point of being helpful. I visited an 86-year-old woman who had enjoyed a very active lifestyle. She had been vibrant, energetic and full of vitality.

Due to a fall, she was bedridden. Her demeanor changed. Her focus was on getting back to where she was. But because she couldn't return to the better times, she was focused on the past.

There comes a time to let go of people. We all know you can't control what another person thinks, says or does, but we sure do try. We want children to take a certain course of action, and they may comply for awhile, but eventually they must find their own direction. I talked to a young lady about some emotional struggles she was facing. Most of her conversation was about people from years ago and things she had done back then. Her past was her present. She couldn't embrace the current moment for fear of what might rear its head up and cause problems for her today.

There comes a time to let go of relationships. You can't control how someone will like, support or encourage. They are who they are. They can learn, but it will come on their time line not yours or anyone else's.

Releasing and Letting Go

The action of letting go is quite simple. It is holding your fist in a tight grip and then slowly letting your fingers release the tension. Emotionally, the process is a little more difficult. We want to hold; we don't want to surrender, and yet surrender may be the most liberating step we can take. It simply means we give up the illusion of control. We don't own any person, event or experience. It or they may be in our lives, but we don't own them. These are moments in time that have passed our way. Our position needs to be one of receiving and releasing.

We receive life as a gift, whether this is a moment of celebration or loss. We sit with the experience or rather let it sit with us for awhile. We listen to it; we learn from it; we let it go. Only when we let it go can we really know the gift of life in its fullness. Life isn't about holding, grasping or owning. It is about receiving, embracing and releasing. These acts run so contrary to our expectations that we find great challenge in seeing the beauty and power of the gift of each one.

Cleaning Out the Junk

My garage reflects my life's journey in many ways. Contained within the four walls of this two-car building, are a collection of memories, intentions, projects and completions. Boxes stored there contain an array of hopes, dreams and mistakes. There is a box with toys from our children's earlier years. There are tools I sometimes use or thought that I would need one day. There are boxes of books. There are partial cans of paint left over from projects in the past. Boards of heart pine salvaged from a church renovation are stacked together in the hopes that one day a table would become a reality. Then, there is just junk—too much to name or begin to list. It is just there—taking up space in what might otherwise be a very useful building.

This parallels my life. I have boxed up and shelved a lot of good intentions, plans and dreams. These someday projects will one day occur when life is easier or better. My desire is to get them out and complete them as I had hoped. You know how the rest of the story goes from there—it never happens. Some of the stuff stored away in my life's attic is too painful to share, not because it is too bad or beyond words—it is beyond experience. In the musical, "Les Miserable," the song, "Empty Chairs at Empty Tables," contains these words:

> *There's a grief that can't be spoken*
> *There's a pain goes on and on*
> *Empty chairs at empty tables*
> *Now my friends are dead and gone.*[xvi]

I heard these for the first time when Dianne and I attended the play on Broadway. I felt a connection in a deep part of my spirit. I do believe there is a grief that can't be spoken. Words fail to capture the depth and width of what has been our experience. You simply cannot take another person to the place where your hurt has lived. Here is why: I don't think you can exchange experiences with another person. You can describe it. You can tell another person where you stood, what happened, and how you felt, but they will not be able to go where you are. It would be like standing on the edge of the Grand Canyon and trying to describe it to someone who is 500 miles away. Unless you stand with the person, see the sights, feel the air, and hear the sounds you will never understand the beauty of this natural wonder. Even then each person may process the moment differently. To say your marriage ended in divorce may strike one person as the greatest tragedy in life because of the deep love and devotion they have given to their relationship. To another, the marriage ended months or years ago and divorce comes as a closure to a source of hurt for them.

To me, this reflects the way that many people try to help other people in a time of need. We try to interpret their moments in life for them. When someone loses a loved one to death, well-meaning friends and family may say, "It was God's will." My response is, "Really? You are saying that it is God's will for the loved one to die because of a drunk driver or due to cancer rather than stay here to spend time with people they love." Mickey Moss, a minister friend, lost his wife, Jane, after her heroic battle with cancer in the winter of 2011. Someone suggested that it was God's will. I loved Mickey's response because of his honesty and directness. He said, "So you are saying that God hates me so much that he took the love of my life away from me?" We don't really think sometimes about what we are saying to those we desire to help.

To heal, I think you need someone to stand with you. It may be a trusted friend, minister, therapist or family member who will sit with you in your moment. Not to tell you how to feel or even suggest a solution at all, but rather to just be present with you. Only when we find someone who loves us enough to be silent, accept and listen from a compassionate yet honest position will we ever find a path to healing. Finding an emotionally safe place gives us permission to get our junk on the table and deal with it. This is a form of YES living. It is saying to another person, YES—you are a person of worth, this is your reality, this is where I hear your hurt or frustration... now where do you want to go from this point forward?

When you find such a relationship, accept it for the gift of grace that it is. These are rare and are to be cherished. When one heart speaks to another heart, then grace has room to flow from one to another, and old wounds and struggles can be released.

You can't clean out all of the junk in an instant. It may take weeks, months or years. For me, it evolved over time. It was a little like cleaning house—I could do a room and then rest for awhile. Then I could go back and clean out another one. There is a matter of timing and readiness to do the work. I call it *soul work*. When you go to the deep places of your spirit where you have been wounded by life or by your own choices, it takes effort and it takes courage. The reward is worth every second of investment. To be free and explore your giftedness in the grace of God allows your life to open up to you. You find your life, and your life finds you. It makes sense, and the pieces fit together into a cohesive whole that leads to a sense of contentment because you are who you need to be and where you need to be.

Straightening Out Crooked Truths

Headed home from a business trip to Pigeon Forge, Tenn., my wife and I decided to take an alternate route. In looking at a map, it appeared Highway 129 just south of Maryville, Tenn., would be a good choice for getting to our destination in North Georgia. Little did we realize the consequence of that one decision. We didn't know that this particular section of highway was named Tail of the Dragon. In one 11 mile section, there are 318 curves. It is designated as America's number one motorcycle and sports car destination because of the beauty and opportunity to navigate so many hills and curves. [xvii]

I have a problem that plagues me on occasion. There are twists and turns with it also. It is very frustrating for me and my family as well. I call it, *having a crooked memory.* This ailment surfaces at unusual times with a variety of consequences. Several years ago, we were at the beach in Destin, Fla., on vacation. We wanted to go out to eat breakfast at a favorite spot. I remembered it was a left-hand turn out of the driveway. My wife, who had visited this same area a few months earlier, knew it was a right-hand turn. I insisted, and went to the left. Wrong direction! This isn't the only example. I recall people acting in prior television shows or movies, but they weren't. I remember parts of conversations. Where it becomes most troublesome is when I remember the wrong facts, or the real facts that I've stored away improperly.

213

Making the wrong turn out of the driveway while on vacation isn't really a big deal. You go down the road, find a place to turn around, and head back in the right direction. I have found a GPS helps those of us who are challenged in finding our way to new destinations. A crooked memory provides inaccurate information for navigating life's forks in the road. We make decisions about the future based upon outdated beliefs. We make choices in relationships due to faulty expectations. We say YES to things we don't even want to do or necessarily like because we are trying to live up to someone else's expectations. We let other people and influences guide us in directions that aren't always in our best interest.

I hold a simple belief. It is one that has been formed by having been a minister for over 40 years. I don't think you can heal your life or ever find a sense of completion or wholeness without addressing the spiritual part of who you are. In making this statement, I want to quickly add that I see a lot of unhealthy faith being presented as healthy. Just because someone goes to church, quotes scripture or presents themselves as a Christian, I do not buy into the idea that it is a healthy connection. Some of the truths that cause our lives to be crooked come from faith.

In the Beginning Was YES!

One of the purposes of the Book of Genesis is to remind us of who gave us life. There are many debates and heated arguments about how and when this took place. For the purpose of this book, I will selectively focus on one thought—In the beginning was YES!

While a thorough and complete study of the first book of the Bible would yield immeasurable thoughts and insights applicable for everyday life, there is one concept that offers support to the idea of Living YES in a NO World! And *YES* was a good word! With each creative act, scripture suggests that God stepped back and looked at it. When he did, there was agreement; "God saw all that he had made, and it was very good." (Genesis 1:31) The act of creation declares the beauty, goodness and design of life. It is to be spent in relationship with God, people and creation. It means each one is to be a steward and to live out a healthy purpose that flows from the very spirit of God. The breath of life is the presence of God within each of us. It is His gift to us, and we are His gift to the world.

What conclusions do I draw from this thought? I am created by the God of this universe. His life flows through every cell in my being. My life is a reflection of his presence. I am something special, not because of *who* I am or *what* I do, but because I am created. I don't add to my value or take away from it. I am His by creation and by design. God's life within me is *His* YES to me. When I give myself to his presence, that *is my* YES to the world! In this freedom, I discover my giftedness and use it to serve the needs of those around me. As a steward of this giftedness, I use it in ways that honor the purpose behind the gift and the one who gave me life.

I love music. I love to listen to it and sing it, though my ability is limited. However, I can hear well enough to know when something is out of tune. I can tell when a note doesn't sound right or is off pitch. If I live my life in harmony with God's gift, then I am in tune with His YES for me. When I choose to live YES, I am embracing all that God has given, I see the good in others, I look for options that lead to growth, hope, love and forgiveness. I give myself to the belief that there is a higher purpose to our lives. I can make a difference. I can choose the response I will make to life no matter what may come my way. I will respond to what I believe to be the presence of God's spirit by opening my heart, mind, emotions, body, and spirit to a positive hope and belief that life is best lived under the guidance of God's spirit.

The Second YES Became Life!

"In the beginning was the word and the word was with God, and the word was God (John 1:1)." There is a theological word used to define this verse. It is called *incarnation*. It is the belief that God became *incarnate* or in the flesh in Jesus Christ. All that he said and did as a person reflects the very nature of God. What does God do? Look at Jesus. What does God want us to know? Listen to Jesus. What kind of life does God want us to live? Follow Jesus. I know this sounds overly simplistic, but there is a basic truth that we need to consider.

Who or what do you use as a model for your life? It may be the goal of becoming successful, happy or blessed. Most likely, you will look at the people you know and see how they live their lives. We then take away a definition—to be successful, I will need to work 80 hours a week. That may or may not be a healthy conclusion. Most of the examples or models we choose to follow will break down over time. You may be successful working 80 hours a week, but is that the way you want to live your life? You may find happiness, but at what price did it come? What have you sacrificed on the altar of happiness to get there?

To me, Jesus offers an example of what it means to live an intentional life. Motivated by an internal compass that related him to his Heavenly Father, he taught, healed, preached and shared compassion with those who needed it the most. That was his mission, and that is what he did totally and completely. He didn't waver in that purpose even when people opposed him. It was who he was, and it was what he did.

I have reflected often on what Jesus did. I believe he came to let us know that God is with us and that God loves us. Yet, there are some additional truths that can be discovered by looking at his life. As he walked his way across Israel, Judea and Samaria, he encountered people. When he did, he stopped and engaged them. On occasion, he healed and taught them. He looked at each one as a person of worth. He saw their condition. He considered who they were as a child of God.

He gave them a voice. To the man who had been ill for 38 years who sat beside the Pool of Bethesda waiting on the waters to be stirred, he asked, "Do you want to be healed?"

This man's word was one of healing, for when asked, he said, "The man who made me well said to me, 'Pick up your mat and walk' (John 5: 11)."

To the woman at the well, he stopped and talked with her—a practice that was out of line with culture and religion, not only because she was a woman, but because of her past. When he promised her "living water," she ran to those she knew and said, "Come, see a man who told me everything I ever did (John 4:29)." Her word was one of forgiveness.

I believe that when life challenges us and comes at us, we are being questioned. We are being tested to the very core of our being. With the question, comes the promise of God's presence and strength. He doesn't prevent the events from coming our way—after all we live a life marked with freedom. Instead, he comes to us (incarnation) and stays with us through the presence of his Spirit. He not only gives us a word, he gives us *our* word. It is the one we most long to hear. It is the one that anchors our soul to his work in our lives. It is the one that most closely connects us to the needs in those around us. For me, that word is YES!

Reconnecting!

With the question comes the need for a relationship. We need and want to be connected to the God of this universe. Knowing how to do that is a challenge for everyone. I don't think that reconnecting to the Divine YES of life is as difficult as we make it seem sometimes. I believe God is the God of revelation. He reveals or makes himself known to us. These many insights into who he is and what he wants us to know are all around us.

While on a retreat several years ago, I heard the expression *means of grace.* I think God uses many means of grace that we might know him better.

One way to reconnect is to listen to your own life. Become a student of *you.* In a sense you become your own life whisperer. Sit quietly with yourself and pay attention to what has happened. Look for recurring themes in pain, relationships or attitudes. Notice where you have grown and where you have become stuck. What does your heart say? What do you think about when you lie down in bed to go to sleep? What do you think about the first thing when you wake up in the morning? Where is your passion for living?

Another good place to start is with Jesus. I find the life of Christ an interesting one to study. It isn't so much what others say about him, but what he said and did while on earth. To me his words speak to the deepest needs of the spirit. When he spoke, he used common and ordinary experiences to reveal deeper wisdom. A parable that begins with "A sower went out to sow," becomes the opportunity to talk about hearing and responding to God's word as lived in the life of Christ. Another one that starts with "A man had two sons," becomes an instrument for talking about forgiveness, resentment and unconditional love. For these reasons, I like to read the parables. These small nuggets of truth lead to deeper insights into the life of Christ and God's message to our world.

I also love the Book of Psalms. To me, the writers offer glimpses into the struggles of our emotional and spiritual landscape. When we are lonely and filled with doubt, Psalm 23 speaks a deep truth in the words, "[1] The LORD is my shepherd, I lack nothing. [2] He makes me lie down in green pastures, he leads me beside quiet waters, [3] he refreshes my soul (Psalm 23:1-3)." Or, when I read in Psalm 139, I am encouraged with the thought, "I praise you because I am fearfully and wonderfully made; your works are wonderful, I know that full well." (Psalm 139: 4) Who hasn't felt the despair of being alone, and wondered like the Psalmist, "Why are you downcast, O my soul? Why so disturbed within me?" (Psalm 42:5)

There were truths Christ tried to reveal and make known about what God wanted and desired for his children. One of the greatest is that you and I are totally and completely loved. From beginning to end, the life of Christ is one consistent message of love.

There are many ways to reconnect, but I recommend quiet prayer that focuses on a conversation with a loving Heavenly Father about the ordinary events of life. I think looking at your attitude toward faith and seeing life as an opportunity to be grateful causes us to see each person and event as a moment of grace. The more we look for the good in ourselves and others, we begin to see more opportunities to say thank you for the gift of now and the many ways we are blessed beyond measure.

The door is open. The time is now. Simply say YES to His Grace and let him reveal that to you in the gift of each moment of every day.

Meeting an Old Friend for the First Time

An Old Truth

In his poem, The Four Quartets, T. S. Eliot shares:

> *With the drawing of this Love*
> *and the voice of this Calling*
> *We shall not cease from exploration*
> *And the end of all our exploring*
> *Will be to arrive where we started*
> *And know the place for the first time.*[xviii]

I have traveled many miles from my beginning days in Northwest Alabama—most, I never anticipated. My journey has been one of exploration from Alabama through Mississippi ultimately to Georgia with a side trip to Kentucky.

It hasn't been the geographical travels and destinations that have defined who I am. Instead, it has been the journey of the spirit. Life was small when I started many, many years ago. I had family. I had a home. I held expectations for an existence defined by being a *Gregg* along Highway 278 near Hamilton, Ala. It grew larger as new places entered the picture and new faces were added to my memory storage bank.

My first years of spiritual formation took place at Poplar Log Freewill Baptist Church. It was a small frame church building where a group of people closely connected by where they lived and what they believed gathered for worship every Sunday morning and evening. Minnie Jewel Cook taught the younger children's Sunday School class. Our lessons were printed on a small post card with a picture on the front and brief lesson on the back. There was always a memory verse to go with the lesson.

We didn't just memorize the verse. As Guy Sayles describes it, "we learned it by heart." [xix] We learned the words and took them to heart. Since the days of Poplar Log, I have stored away many, many pieces of information. I have earned degrees, written books, preached sermons, developed training material, delivered innumerable leadership presentations, and traveled untold miles. Life grew larger, but it also grew smaller.

I keep coming back to where I started and discovering an old truth all over again. The reality of God's love for me keeps shining through in a multitude of ways. I knew this message 50 years ago, but it is as though I am experiencing it again for the first time. An old truth becomes a new one when we must relearn it to face a different experience or phase of life.

An Old Friend

I can say the same thing for meeting an old friend again for the first time. In his book, "The Active Life: A Spirituality of Work, Creativity and Caring," the author, Parker J. Palmer[xx], includes a passage of scripture from the Gospel of Mark:

> *35 Very early in the morning, while it was still dark, Jesus got up, left the house and went off to a solitary place, where he prayed. 36 Simon and his companions*

went to look for him, [37] and when they found him, they exclaimed: "Everyone is looking for you!"

[38] Jesus replied, "Let us go somewhere else—to the nearby villages—so I can preach there also. That is why I have come." (Mark 1:35-38)

I like the idea of going to a solitary place to pray. I can relate to being alone and quiet. I can understand the feeling of "Everyone is looking for you."

There is one thought that stood out for me more than others. I kept coming back to: "Let us go somewhere else—to the nearby villages—so I can preach there also. That is why I have come." I couldn't put these words in context with what had taken place earlier; baptism of Jesus; call of disciples; healing of sick; and "all of the people coming to him."

Over time, I have come to see this passage in a new light. Jesus was called to be the person that he was. He was internally motivated to fulfill a mission. His work was based upon who he was and what he had been given to do, not upon the popularity of the crowds or even the expectations of those who were closest to him. In this context, he lived with intention. There was a purpose to his life that couldn't be explained or even completely understood. It was who he was and what he was on this earth to do.

This single passage has done more to shape my life than any other. I find in it many thoughts for inspiration and encouragement. Here are a few to consider:

I find encouragement to be me. No one can live their life guided by the expectations of the crowd or even those you consider to be your closest supporters. Me to be *me*—or you to be *you*—may be a great gift to our world.

I hear courage to live authentically. To be who you are as a person will go contrary to most of the world. We don't have many versions of authenticity to use as a role model.

I hear courage to live with intention. It requires strength to listen for a different voice, walk to a different drum beat and live a different message.

A New Life

Healing takes place when we give up the illusions. Those that are inherited, borrowed, or absorbed from the culture around us soon lose their luster. We may believe success will lead to happiness, when in reality it may lead to more problems. Ask anyone who has found success, and you may be surprised to learn that happiness did not arrive as a byproduct. I have bought into my share of illusions. Call them a *fantasy* or *mirage*, the results were the same. I thought that if I moved to a bigger church life would be better. It wasn't. There were more people, but there were more problems as well.

I thought that if I served the church, people would love me. I have had wonderful people and lasting relationships from every church I have served. In any situation though, there are people who will only give out affection and acceptance as long as you do what they expect you to do. Fortunately these were limited in number but still serve as a healthy reminder that you can't live your life based upon what you think other people will do for you.

I thought I could be perfect. I know... what a disappointment, but this one has always been tied to my need for acceptance. There came a time though when I realized I couldn't do it, and it was a waste of energy to even try. The day

I laid down the mantel of perfectionism was a wonderful day of celebration. I tell people now I am a recovering perfectionist.

When I gave up the illusions, I realized I am just *me*. I have rediscovered old truths. I have met an old friend again for the first time. I have come back to where I started. It is my place in the world. I will live it the best that I know how.

Creating a Healthy Place

The ABC television show, "Extreme Home Makeover[xxi]," was filmed in Madison, Ga., the week of July 11-16, 2011. The producers selected 9-year-old Anaiah Tucker and her family to be the recipients of a new home. This came as a great surprise to this rising fourth grader who pushed her 5-year-old sister out of the path of an oncoming truck only to be severely injured herself. In seven days, Anaiah and her family had a new home completely built from the ground up. For them, it offers an opportunity to enjoy a home with features specifically designed for her special physical needs.

We may not have the resources or expertise to do what the producers of the television show were able to do, but we can build a place where life is designed for our specific needs. I think every moment of every day we are creating our place in this world. We create ones filled with YES, hope and possibilities, or we create ones of NO, can't and limitations. I know a senior adult who was hurt by life many years ago; she still lives in a house of pain. Unfortunately, she hasn't worked through the hurt so it has built walls, a roof and a floor around her. You can't see her or talk to her without noticing that it still bubbles beneath the surface of who she is. With every word and action, she continues the ache from an event that happened years ago. She builds a place where pain can live each day.

After a while, you grow weary of living with the NO that life sends you or the one you generate for yourself. I grew tired of trying to be a perfectionist. It just didn't work for me or anyone around me. So, I began to build a different environment—one where mistakes were accepted; good was substituted for perfect; and getting something done today was better than waiting to get it done perfectly tomorrow.

Say YES

I love the word *YES*. It opens doors, creates opportunities, and gives permission to the influences that make us stronger and allows greater contentment of spirit. Guided by an intentional purpose, we release the energy of talent and passion we possess in a direction that makes a difference and allows us to live a life that matters. There are words that fuel YES for me.

Forgiveness: There comes a time when you have to forgive yourself and others. Hurt enters our lives unexpectedly and without invitation. Every time it does we lose something— a hope, a dream or a relationship. Or, we do something that is less than our best self. It is easy to hang onto the hurt and let it fester in our spirit, robbing us of joy and peace. At some point, you decide to forgive. That one decision releases the floodgates of stored up negative emotions that have held you captive for minutes, days or years. It isn't a matter of agreeing with what happened as much as acceptance of the reality that letting go of the hurt is the emotionally mature thing to do.

Healing: Healing takes place when we realize our life is a gift to us, God, and those around us. We learn to cherish who we are—personality, talent, interest, past, hurt, forgiveness, inconsistencies, joys, celebration, hope and dreams. We find joy in who we are and find pleasure in being alive—motivated by the gift of being alive and engaged with the people around us. Then we can see where each twist and turn in our story has added another chapter to who we are—we are richer, deeper and wiser for what we have experienced.

Wholeness: Our life only makes sense when we see that it has become a cohesive picture. The questions that have plagued you suddenly add meaning to the journey. Why did I take that job in Phoenix that was so far away from family? Why did I lose the love of my life? Why did I major in English instead of Engineering? Why didn't I go to college when I had the opportunity? In the past, you may have punished yourself with these unanswerable questions. We aren't mind readers, clairvoyants or magicians. We are everyday, ordinary people. We make choices and decisions. We follow a course believing it is the right one.

Saying YES doesn't make anything take place, but it does remind me that I have a choice in how I will live my life. I choose to live it with zest, energy, passion, intention and purpose. I don't live it perfectly. Sometimes I fail miserably. I often struggle, but never want to forget the decision to live YES.

Embrace NO

NO is a wonderful word. It sets limits, establishes boundaries and stops action. Guided by an intentional purpose, this word allows us to keep our focus on top priorities. Used without thought or reflection, it becomes nothing more than a weather vane that guides us in the direction of public opinion. Our lives are worth a healthy NO. We are alive and gifted. We have the right, privilege and responsibility to set limits on ourselves and others.

Honesty

To me being healthy means I will strive to be honest with myself, reality and life. If I am—and that is a battle for everyone—I will have to confess that being healthy is an on-going journey of the spirit. I don't think you ever arrive at a time and location that allows you to say, "I am totally and completely healthy." Instead, I strive to be strong, but my strength doesn't come from a title, possessions or personal power. I am a searcher for truth even when that is truth about my need to masquerade, hide and pretend. I often want to send my impostor out into the world so that others will see the good person or well intentioned person that I want them to see.

Finding your healthy place is an ongoing journey. It changes as life, circumstances and people change. It must be negotiated over and over again. I know that I am healthy when I take ownership of my story. I am the author of every word. We often don't get to write what we thought we would write with our life, but we do get to edit the story as events and experiences come to us. The words that go on the page of my experience are ones that have come from the deep parts of my soul. This is where I dwell when I live an intentional life. I am not held hostage by any event or person from the past. I am free to see the good and the bad as threads in one seamless garment. I look for ways to celebrate the gift of me—not in an egocentric or self-centered way, but with deep appreciation and affection. I don't have to defend my limitations or penalize my giftedness. I live with gratitude the moments of grace that I am allowed to share.

When I am healthy I will speak and live YES with intention. When I speak and live NO, I do so for the purpose of drawing boundaries that protect yet nurture my mission in life. When you are healthy emotionally, mentally and spiritually, you will come from a different place. It is your place. You have created it as you have done your soul work. You know what it takes to face reality. You know the pain of loss. You know what was required to develop your sense of home. You know hurt. You know healing. You will not think, talk, act or dream like the crowd. Your thoughts will originate from you and your relationship to your Heavenly Father. You will listen for the still small voice of the Spirit. You will see your soul as who you are. You will hold the tension between what could be and what really is. You will be on a journey that is more focused on being alive, present and open than arriving at some future destination.

You are creating a place for you to be *you*, listening for the words you have been given to hear, and speaking the message you have been given to share. This is your healthy place. You protect it with YES and NO—words you have learned so speak and live.

Sacred Stories

We Held Her

In March 2010, my husband, Wade, and I found out we were expecting a baby. This exciting news came despite health issues on my part and following months of trying and many prayers. My pregnancy progressed normally. We were excited to go for our 20-week appointment and sonogram on June 1, 2010. "It's a girl," the sonographer said. After moving all over my bulging belly for about 20 minutes, she told me I could get dressed and wait to see the doctor. The doctor came in and explained to us that everything looked good, though they couldn't see all of Eve's heart. He explained that it may have been the way she was positioned. As a precaution, she referred us to a perinatologist, whom we would see the next week.

We decided to name our little girl Evelyn Elizabeth, after her great-grandmother and her grand mommy. To shorten her name we would call her Eve. We tried to remain calm and positive though we prayed with almost every breath we took as we waited to see the new doctor. I remember every important date of my pregnancy because they are etched in my mind and heart.

On July 7, 2010, we met with the perinatologist. My world crumbled as he described a heart defect that Eve might possess. It was called Hypoplastic Left Heart Syndrome. This meant the left side of her heart was underdeveloped, and she would require open heart surgery within the first week of her life just to survive. At first, I wanted to strike out at the doctor in anger...and then I wanted to die. In my head, I began to ask God why he did this to

232

us, our baby and our family. I couldn't comprehend anything after the doctor used the words heart defect. *He indicated that I would continue to see my regular OB/GYN until I reached 32 weeks in my pregnancy, and then he would take over my care. He also wanted us to meet the cardiologists and surgeons who would be taking care of Eve once she was born and transferred to a children's hospital.*

In September, we traveled for more scans and to meet the surgeon, one of the top pediatric cardiothoracic surgeons in the country. He was very thorough. He went into detail about Eve's defect, how severe it was, and even detailed the surgery for us. We learned that it would be about an eight-hour procedure. He was quite positive, telling us the mortality rate for HLHS in this day in time is quite low, somewhere around eight to ten percent. During this visit, we toured the hospital and the Cardiac Intensive Care Unit, where Eve would be cared for once she was born. We also got to see babies who had recently had heart surgery and meet their families so we would know about what to expect.

After a routine doctor's appointment on October 7, I was hospitalized due to preeclampsia. At this point, we still had not packed the suitcase or the car. After a day in the hospital, I convinced my doctor to let me go home—I had baby showers to attend! Over the next two weeks, I attended three of my four baby showers. We had no room to put anything due to the volume of gifts we received. Once everything was washed, pressed and put away, we finally packed. Knowing we would go to the children's hospital once Eve was born, we packed enough clothes to last us at least a month.

Monday, October 18, I went in for my 36-week checkup, and though I tried to be convincing, I wasn't lucky enough to get out of the hospital stay this time. My doctor told us to walk over to labor and delivery, because we would be having a baby in the next day or two. Eve didn't come on our timeline, so Wednesday evening when our doctor visited he told us we would be having a baby the next morning, and if I wanted anything to eat, I needed to get it before midnight. Thank goodness for my husband, some quarters and vending machines—hello, soft drink and candy bar!

After just a few hours sleep, I was moved to a delivery room around 6 a.m. Scared to death, I asked for 15 minutes of complete peace and quiet: no nurses, no doctors, nobody. My labor nurse was the most wonderful nurse I've ever met. She actually stood outside my door and wouldn't let anyone in during those 15 minutes.

One of the resident doctors came in and explained to me how the next few hours would go: they would break my water, start medications and fluids, and then administer an epidural. An epidural was a major priority for me, and thanks to my nurse I would have it ASAP. She even wrote "Epidural ASAP" on my chart. After 10 hours, I was ready to start pushing. Wade was a wonderful partner, encouraging me every minute. And after only 20 minutes, Eve was here.

Eve was beautiful. She weighed 5 pounds 9.4 ounces, 19 inches of pure perfection with beautiful, soft brown hair. She didn't make a peep. She was fine, obviously just laid back and relaxed like her Daddy. I finally got to hold her five minutes after she was born, and then she was taken to the NICU. They had to immediately start an umbilical IV line with medications to keep her patent ductus arteriosus (PDA) open—this was critical to her survival until she could have her surgery. A few hours later I was finally able to go to the NICU to see her. She was sleeping with what seemed to be an enormous pacifier in her mouth; it was as wide as her face! She was so warm when I held her hand and touched her. We sat next to her for a while. I couldn't stop staring at her. She was so beautiful.

The next morning, the nursing staff had Eve ready to leave for the children's hospital and brought her to me so I could see her before they left. I heard them coming down the hallway, that big, ugly contraption they had her in made so much noise. I guess it was a portable incubator type thing. I reached through the small hand holes and told her I would see her later. I wouldn't be released until Saturday because my blood pressure was still too high. My Mom stayed with me that night, while Wade and his mom traveled to be with Eve. Before 5 o'clock Saturday morning, I already had a shower, fixed my hair, and had my makeup on. I called the nurses and told them to bring my discharge papers so I could leave. This Mama was in one big hurry!

It seemed like a lifetime before I got to the children's hospital, but once I got there I couldn't get to the Cardiac Intensive Care Unit fast enough. I finally saw her, and the nurse couldn't even finish getting "Do you want to hold her?" out of her mouth before I said, "yes." Eve was so tiny and perfect. I still don't understand how something could've been wrong with her. She was so quiet, and only cried when Wade and I changed her diaper. She was definitely not a fan of diaper changes!

Eve remained in the CICU for several days until the doctors and surgeons could examine her and come up with plans and schedules for surgery. Wade and I dreaded the day we went in and they had a date set. That day came and her surgery was scheduled for Tuesday, October 26. She would be the second case that day, so her surgery would start around 11 a.m.

Wade and I were able to go into the CICU early that day and spend time with her. We held her for a few hours, certainly not *long enough, but I'm thankful for every second. We walked her down to the operating room and told her, "See you later." I think that was the longest day of my life. Our families were there with us, along with our pastors. We were escorted to the surgical waiting room, where the OR nurse would call every hour to update us. I believe it was around 8 p.m. when we got the call they were closing her up and getting ready to take her back to the CICU. The surgeon came to the waiting room and explained that he thought the surgery went well and that we would be able to see Eve in about an hour.*

Even though we had seen babies that had already had surgery, I had no idea what to expect. My perfect little baby girl still had an opening in her chest, covered with a clear bandage. There were tubes and wires coming from every single part of her body. The incision was a few inches long and the width of the opening was about an inch. We could actually see her tiny heart beating through the bandage. Parents were allowed in the CICU as long as doctors weren't making rounds. This rule made for lots of long days and nights. Then Wade and I figured out a schedule. We would go mid-mornings and stay until afternoon. Then we would go back to the nearby Ronald McDonald house where we were staying to take a nap and eat, and then go back to the hospital until early evening and stay until midnight or so.

A few days passed. Eve was stable and doing well. Wade went home for a few days to take care of some things at work and home. My Mom stayed with Eve and me. Eve was apparently doing well, but she had some swelling that they couldn't figure out.

On Monday, November 1, Wade was working more than two hours away, and the nurse called me back to the CICU. It seemed Eve had a blood clot in one of her major arteries preventing the

236

blood from circulating down from her head to the rest of her body. Instead of taking her to the cath lab, they decided to take her back to surgery to remove the clot.

I grabbed Mama, and we walked Eve back down to surgery. I called Wade and told him to come back to Atlanta. I don't know how fast he drove, but he was there before Eve came out of surgery. This time she had a different surgeon, and he explained to us that he had removed the clot and Eve should be fine. The next few hours and days revealed that Eve was not fine; the swelling wasn't going down and her skin color changed. We knew that Eve wasn't well. Later, we were informed that Eve had another blood clot.

Late on the night of Wednesday, November 3, my mama was sitting with Eve while Wade and I rested for a few hours. She called and said Eve's blood pressure had dropped, that the nurses were having trouble keeping it stable. So Wade and I rushed over to the hospital. I saw a crash cart and tons of doctors and nurses at Eve's bedside. Our family was there with us. We all sat down, watching, praying and crying. An hour or two later, a doctor came over and said, "Eve isn't doing well. Basically, we are keeping her from dying." At that point, Wade and I asked our family to let us have a few minutes.

Eve's nurse came over and asked what we wanted to do and offered us some options...We knew it was Eve's time...that God wanted her to come live with him. I sat there and begged Him to take me instead.

We decided to take Eve off the life-support machine, and our decision was to hold her while she went to live with her Heavenly Father. The nurses turned off all the monitors, removed all the tubes, wires and lines and handed Eve to me. Wade and I talked to her, kissed her and told her how much we loved her and that *we would all be together again one day, and that one day she would get to meet her sister. We explained to her that she was going to a place where she would be happy and healthy, where she could play all day with her great-grandparents and her Uncle Jeremiah, where there isn't any wrong-doing, the skies are always sunny, and the streets are paved with gold. We asked her to watch over us and her sister. And then she was gone...We continued to hold her. I couldn't cry. I didn't have any tears left in my body. All I could tell her was, "I'm sorry I couldn't fix it, Baby."*

I don't know how long we were there; I think it was around 2 a.m. at this point. I was in shock that we had to make the decision to let our daughter die at two weeks of age. The next few hours and days were a blur. I remember going to the store to pick out an outfit for Eve to wear for her burial. She wore a smocked, pink and white gingham shirt and long bloomers, with white bow in her hair. I remember getting the phone call from the funeral home that they had gotten Eve ready and we could come see her. I don't remember the visitation or her funeral.

As parents, we instinctively protect our children, but we couldn't protect Eve. Grief is a horrible experience. It has been a year since Eve died, a year of constant depression, sadness, relentless anger, guilt and resentment for me. I have decent days, and I have terrible days. I have questioned God, and I have cursed God. Babies aren't supposed to die. Every single day seems like it all happened yesterday. I went to church for the first time since Eve died on June 12, and less than a week after that, my Mom died. And let me tell you, losing a child and losing a parent do not compare. Both losses are jarring in different ways. Suffering both of these losses in less than a year has been almost unbearable. A single day doesn't pass that I don't cry. My faith and beliefs over the past two years have certainly been

questioned, and on some days they are still questioned. I have YES days, and I have NO days. If not for the love and support of my husband, Wade, I probably wouldn't be here today writing this. He is my YES in life. I don't want to live without Eve and Mama, but I know, regardless of how my head thinks, God knows what I feel in my heart, and I will be with them again one day.
~*Kacey Lowe Dixon*

Start with the End in Mind

When my oldest child was almost four, he was diagnosed with autism and severe Attention Deficit Hyperactivity Disorder (ADHD) or I should say "we" were diagnosed. He couldn't communicate his needs and wants, had very few words, isolated himself from others and had obsessive and compulsive behaviors. He played with weird objects and only liked Mattel cars—he could sit for hours on end watching the wheels turn as he pushed them on the floor. He threw tantrums all the time, mainly due to his lack of language, and was just simply in his own little world.

The diagnosis, although much needed, was still a complete shock. At that time my third child was only two weeks old. As we listened to the neurologist's details of the diagnosis, it seemed like a very harsh and grim label for a child, and he would never be the child we had hoped he would be. He said, "Have you ever seen Rain Man? Do you know what autism is? My recommendation to you would be to place him in a special needs school. He may never communicate like others, and you need to get him therapy."

And that was it! We had waited months and months for this visit with the neurologist only for him to say this and send us on *our way. The diagnosis painted a very difficult life for my child—seemed as if he would always be in his own world.*

I cried for days on end. I was heartbroken and had a feeling of total helplessness. Although the diagnosis was needed, it was also very devastating. I knew my child was different and wanted to know why, but it seemed all so very real at that time, and I had no direction of where to go and what to do for him. Dreams and hopes seemed to have vanished and we were now living a completely different life. I had thoughts of, "Why me God and why my child?" My child wasn't dying, but yet I was mourning—mourning the loss of what could have been. Doubt and eventually anger would take over my life.

After two weeks of tears and total depression, I began what you could call a crusade *of sorts. I had prayed day and night asking why but mainly asking for direction from God. I was completely determined that I wasn't going to let a diagnosis, label or what professionals said to get in the way of me helping my child. I had no idea at the time it would take years to see major results. When people told me what my child wouldn't be able to do, I think it ignited a fire in my soul, and I became determined to do whatever I could to help him have a better life.*

I knew there had to be other moms out there like me who could offer encouragement, listen or give me guidance on where to begin. I looked for encouragement and found it in scripture. First Thessalonians 5:11 says, "Therefore encourage one another and build each other up, just as in fact you are doing." As I talked to moms, I did find the support I was seeking and the best advice I was given was to, "Get Busy. If you want your son to be able to learn to communicate and function as a productive citizen when he is an adult, do what you can now." I'll never forget those words.

Get busy *meant to find the therapy my child needed. It also meant turning our home into a therapy facility. Results were great for kids with autism who received therapy at an early age. Children with autism could learn like other children, it was just going to take hours and hours, days and days and years and years of therapy. How can anyone limit what a child can do? I am a realist but also a believer. I believed in my son and also believed that God could direct me and knew he didn't give me anything I couldn't handle.*

We began therapy 40 hours a week. My son was going to speech therapy, occupational therapy for fine motor delays, physical therapy for low muscle tone issues, hippo therapy (therapy on horseback), aquatic therapy, social skills therapy, music therapy and the list goes on and on. If I discovered a new therapy, we would at least give it a try. We went to numerous professionals and even to a homeopathic doctor who placed him on supplements. The poor kid must have been so tired, and I was completely exhausted. The doubt and fear continued to haunt me, but I wasn't angry. We began to see some small improvements as the months went by.

I also began to attend several workshops and seminars and search on the Internet to teach myself how to care for my son. I can't remember exactly who said this to me, but it was also one of the driving forces that kept me going: "Begin with an end in mind". I really didn't know the significance of those words when my child was only four. I eventually learned that, "Begin with an end in mind," meant letting nothing stand in the way of helping my son, never accepting no for an answer and not accepting can't or won't, and always having a dream of what he could be as an adult. This passage on perseverance would come to mean so much to me years later when I was reminded of it by a great friend.

James 1: 2-8 reads:

"Consider it pure joy, my brothers, whenever you face trials of many kinds, because you know that the testing of your faith develops perseverance. Perseverance must finish its work so that you may be mature and complete, not lacking anything. If any of you lacks wisdom, he should ask God, who gives generously to all without finding fault, and it will be given to him. But when he asks, he must believe and not doubt, because he who doubts is like a wave of the sea, blown and tossed by the wind. That man should not think he will receive anything from the Lord he is a double-minded man, unstable in all he does."

I began to see my experience as more than a setback; it became a spiritual journey as well.

My son did attend a year at a special needs preschool. He made significant gains in life skills but still needed help in social skills. We made a very unconventional (at the time) decision to place him in a regular pre-kindergarten with typical peers. Some people may have thought I was doing him an injustice, but I truly believed it was the only way to gain social skills. He would remain in a regular education classroom with support and therapy at school.

Each year since that decision, he has gained more and more skills and worked his way to independence and academic success. What seemed to be a lifetime to develop certain skills, has been nothing less than a miraculous recovery. Today my son is a sixth grader in honors classes. He is only receiving consultative services at school, mainly due to the lack of organizational skills. He is not receiving any therapy of any kind. Although he still has his quirks, most wouldn't even know he ever had a diagnosis. He brightens our days with his humorous ways and ability to make everyone smile and love him. He is the manager of the middle school football team and is showing cattle at 4-H and state shows. He has great grades, many friends and is quite a social butterfly.

Although it was a very difficult but very rewarding journey, I always had to believe we would overcome autism. I have become a parent who listens and encourages other newly diagnosed parents. I believe God gave me my son to teach me and to make me feel closer to him. I don't believe he created my son with autism but rather when my child developed autism, God gave me the knowledge and wisdom to be able to get my child what he needed. 1 Corinthians 13:13 says ..."faith, hope and love. But the greatest of these is love." I always had faith that God would provide and lead me to do the right thing. Hope was what drove me to continue to believe we would overcome autism one day. There is no other love like the love for a child. I have been truly blessed to have three incredible children. Autism has become an important part of our lives and has taught us many great things. We have learned compassion, sympathy and to never give up hope. We are truly grateful to God for giving us the strength to keep persevering.

~Brenda Knight Smith

Taking Over My Whole Being

I could feel it taking over my whole being again. The crippling fatigue that the nasty disease of depression leaves as its calling card was once again moving within my being. As I sat on the front porch watching my children play, I felt so detached. They had asked me to play so many times but I could not get my body to move. I wanted to scream, "Why is this happening again, God?" I could feel the tears well up again. They had become frequent, unwelcome visitors. Weight had begun to pile on physically and emotionally.

The woman I was becoming was night and day different from the young, vibrant woman I used to be. In the past I had a hunger for life! I would laugh and engage others and yearn for the day my children would ask me to run and play with them. What had changed? What had taken that vibrant woman and turned her into a gray, lifeless shell? Really, there were two things; depression and buying into the word NO. How many times do we hear that word from the moment we are born? How many times do we believe the lie that no is the final answer and how many times do we use that word as an excuse?

The biggest NO I bought into was when I initially became a mother. The visions I had once entertained of being this doting, capable mother vaporized soon after the birth of our first child, our precious daughter. I had heard of the baby blues many new moms experienced, and I hoped that the bad thoughts and feelings I had were simply a quaint and fleeting bout of baby blues. As months went by and the indescribable thoughts and feelings didn't dissipate but continued to strengthen, I knew in my heart what I was experiencing was much deeper and more

244

troublesome than a case of the blues. But I had bought into the lie that, "good mothers, good women, blessed women don't get depressed." And most importantly, "no one can know what you are experiencing because you will be considered an inadequate mother and wife." At that point in time, post-partum depression was beginning to be recognized for the debilitating condition it can b, but the stigma of depression I felt was not diminished at all.

So, what did I do? I hid behind a happy face, pretended outwardly that all was fine and did my best to pretend that those silly blues had faded. I bought totally and completely into the NO of the shame of depression. I prayed, struggled inwardly, cried alone and made some pretty bad decisions as I wrestled with this NO in my world—No, I wasn't worthy of the help I so desperately needed, because what would people think? Even telling a doctor would be admitting the problem, and that was just not something I could do. Good mothers and wives didn't have these problems.

When I became pregnant with our second child, we were on the verge of a cross-country move. My situation hadn't changed. I still struggled each and every moment with the crippling thoughts and feelings I'd had. What had changed though was my choice to accept the particular NO of confessing my problem. I made it a point to talk with my new doctor in our new state about the experiences I'd had after the birth of our daughter, what I was still experiencing and discuss the options available to me after the birth of this second child, our son. Though my doctor seemed somewhat skeptical, he listened to my concerns, and after the birth of my son, we tried a few different medications until we found one that seemed to help. Finally, I had released myself from the chains of that particular NO. I had *chosen YES to seek help! Finally, a solution was here... so I thought.*

That particular medication did wonders as far as keeping the worst of the depression at bay, at least for a while. We got past the baby blues time period and I felt comfortable staying on the medication a bit longer. Around the time our son was 3, I wanted to quit taking the medication. After all, "Good mothers shouldn't have to be on medications, right?" Under my doctor's supervision, I began to wean away from the anti-depressant that had helped me so much. I seemed to be ok for a while, but the negative thoughts and mind-numbing fatigue became ever-present, and my zest for life was gone.

This is where I was on that spring day on my front porch. I was watching my children play, exhausted to my very core, wanting desperately to get up and enjoy them, but I simply couldn't move. I was now nearly 20 pounds overweight and was ragged with the feelings of failure, because I needed the help of medication when God had chosen to bless me with such a fantastic family.

It was within a few weeks of this particular day that a good friend and I were talking about an exercise program she was doing. Mind you, I had tried exercise numerous times to combat the weight and overcome the fatigue. I had, however, also bought into the NOs of, "When you exercise you take time away from your family. It's selfish to desire that time for mind and body renewal." As a good mother, your first priority is to your family, and your needs usually come at the end of that list. And finally and most fatally, "No, you aren't worthy of taking the time to focus on physical healing." Despite these NO's however, I listened with a great deal of interest to my friend's experience with this exercise program. She was a mom, a wife, a daughter, a co-worker, and a sister in the faith. She was all the things I was but was saying YES to taking care of herself! I could see my YES on the horizon.

Before long, I purchased the exercise program my friend had described to me. With the help of my sweet, supportive husband (who had also found his journey to YES through the form of exercise and good nutrition), I made time to exercise each morning before the rest of the family woke up. We made room in our budget for a meal supplement that provided the vitamins and minerals my body so desperately needed. Creating room in our budget for this was a YES in and of itself, because I had also bought into the lie that I wasn't worthy of spending this type of money on something to help me get better.

So many YES opportunities! Choosing the YES of the benefits of a healthy life both physically and mentally was, oddly enough, difficult. I had believed the lies of NO for so long that I felt guilty for taking time for myself, spending money on things that could help me, and creating opportunities for healing mentally and physically. I had believed that taking time from my family to exercise (what a silly type of NO) would be selfish, that wanting to look and feel better was a shameful form of narcissism. In contrast to these NOs I encountered so many YES opportunities. I discovered that saying YES to a healthier lifestyle meant more YES time for my family such as "Yes, kids, I will get up and play with you because now I have the energy." I even said YES to becoming an Independent Coach through the company that provided the workout and supplement!

Saying YES to taking care of the body God had given me opened the door to so many other YES opportunities. In July of 2011, the biggest YES of this particular journey came to fruition: I became a certified personal trainer. Me, the woman who could barely move at times, who could barely motivate herself to exercise in the beginning, who would spend so much time crying and hurting, was on a journey to help and motivate others!

I have learned, through this journey to YES that we have to be open to the opportunities we've been blessed with and to the wisdom of friends we encounter along the way. I have learned we have to forget about the chains of NO that held us back in the past and grasp firmly to the hope of now that a firm and resolute YES provides. Most importantly, I have learned that saying YES to health allows us to serve in the way we were intended to serve, to live the purpose we were created to fulfill. We have been given one life to lead, one opportunity to make it count and to help others make it count along the way. I've learned that saying YES will open the doors to new adventures, new friendships and new opportunities to live our God-given lives to the fullest!

We are bombarded with NO opportunities daily when it comes to health: Will I choose to take a few extra minutes to prepare a healthy meal instead of going through the drive-thru again? Will I take a few extra moments to care for the body and mind God has given me, or will I choose to watch a little more television? Will I choose to believe the lies of shame that are thrown my way, or will I look toward the future with a renewed sense of self and hope? Will I take the opportunities given me to encourage and motivate others, or will I hide behind the light I've been given to shine?

I look back at the woman who was so lifeless, so down and in so much pain (though no one really knew) and I am sad that she lived the lies of NO for so long. I'm sad that she did everything she could to find her path to happiness, going down all the wrong side roads along the way. Mostly, though, I am grateful to have found the acceptance, the beauty, the love and the zest for

this life we've been blessed with through the courageous choice of saying YES to a healthier existence.
   ~Anonymous

A Faraway Look in His Eyes

My name is Jan Coker, my husband's name is Warren, and we live in Georgia. I work from home and my husband works as a Unit Manager for Walker State Prison in Rock Spring. We were married in March of 1977, and like all other young married couples we had plans of having a good career, buying a home and starting a family. In 1979 we started on plans of building our home, but I found out I was pregnant and we were so excited to be having our first child!

Kevin Derek Coker was born at 12:08 pm on March 24, 1980, weighing only five pounds. He had the darkest hair and was so tiny. They took him straight away, and I really didn't get a chance to see him very well. I wondered what was going on because they were all scurrying around, and it was making me very uncomfortable and scared.

They pushed me in the hallway, and a doctor came to me and told me that Kevin was going to be sent to a Children's Hospital because they suspected he had a heart problem and a problem with his esophagus. My happiness immediately became devastation; I was terrified and in shock. I remember thinking, what in the world have I ever done that was so bad to have this happen to me? I knew that Kevin's problems didn't have anything to do with whether or not I had done something wrong, but my mind was really working overtime. This was my first *child, and I didn't know all about taking care of baby, much less one with so many problems. It seemed like I was being punished.*

The first few years with Kevin were really hard for him and for us since we spent lots of days in and out of the hospital. The first surgery was immediately following his birth to repair an esophageal fistula. He had to have a stomach tube inserted so we could feed him. He was not eating by mouth very well due to the surgical procedure. He came home from the hospital a few days later, and we headed to Atlanta to a heart specialist. He was diagnosed with a condition called Tetrology of Fallot, *which meant more surgeries to come. Some of those surgeries were temporary, due to the fact that the arteries were really small and they needed a chance to grow a little bigger so that they could perform a corrective surgery. We were also told that boys with this type of heart problem usually didn't live more than five years. I just felt that Kevin would make it longer than that. I will say it is hard to be positive with so many negatives in the way, but when you reach a point of something so devastating, the only thing you have to hold on to is God and his mercy and love. That is what keeps you going.*

Over the next several years, Kevin underwent many temporary heart operations and several heart catheterizations. Little did we know that the stomach tube would become a permanent body part for him—we could not get him to eat by mouth, and there was no apparent reason for it except that he was unable to eat following the esophageal surgery. Doctors seemed to think it was more psychological than physical, because he never got to experience eating by mouth at birth to develop his taste buds. This was a work in progress for me. I would try everything to get him to eat, but no matter what I did, he just would not take anything by mouth. Finally, I had to actually stop feeding him with the tube so that he would get hungry enough to want something to eat. The first thing he ever ate by mouth was a saltine cracker, and I will never forget the excitement over that one little cracker. It was only a few bites but for me it was as if he had eaten an entire meal!

Gradually as he grew and got stronger, he would eat different things, mostly spicy foods. I guess it took something with a strong flavor for him to really be able to taste it. By the time he was 5 and ready to start kindergarten, the tube was out, and he was eating fairly well but still small for his age due to the heart problem. He started kindergarten and went for half the year for the first year to get used to it. He did well, but still got sick a lot since he had not been around a lot of kids other than in the hospital. We held him back that year and let him start kindergarten again the next year, and he did very well. He was really smart, and he loved being social. He had developed a unique personality, but the one thing that was most unique about Kevin was his love for God. I am so thankful that I raised him in church, because I wanted him to know of God's love and that he was special to him and to us.

There were times when we were in the hospital and he was going through all the needle sticks for blood work, all the tests, all the operations and so many people doing so many things to him, that he would get so tired of it all. I know he was so scared—I was even scared, always fearing the worst every time we went. Through it all, he maintained his positive attitude. Even though he knew he was limited with his physical activity, he was happy. I do remember one time when he was getting ready to go to the hospital for a heart cath, he was sitting in the floor with me and we were talking about it. He started crying and he said to me, "Mom I wish I was like Adam or Seth and could do *more things like them." It broke my heart—how do you answer a statement like that?*

I answered him with the only thing I knew to be true, I said, "Kevin, never ever wish you were like someone else, be proud of how God made you, because he made you this way for a reason, and we have to accept that God knows what he is doing, and one day we will know that reason. You may not realize it but you are touching people's lives every day by the way you live and handle things."

We sat there and cried, and he said, "OK, Mom, I will be proud of who I am!" I never loved him more than at that moment!

Kevin also had a problem with the platelets in his blood. This is what helps the blood to clot when you have a wound. We had to get platelet counts on a routine basis, and his were dropping so much that his doctors put him on steroids to build them up. That worked fairly well and he started gaining weight—he was eating really well too. And he was doing well in school and had actually caught up with his age group.

He was just turning 11, and because we had held him back a couple of years due to his health problems he was just finishing third grade. He had a really good summer, and things were looking up. He went for a checkup and a heart cath during the summer, and we were told that he was big enough and strong enough to undergo the corrective surgery on his heart. In August he was on oxygen while at home to prepare for the surgery, so he wasn't able to start school at the beginning of the year. The surgery was scheduled for October 2 of 1991. He kept in touch with his classmates by making videos to send to school, and in return they would make one to send to him to let him know what they were doing. He was getting his assignments and a teacher was coming around to work with him while he was homebound.

The day before his corrective surgery, Kevin was very quiet and didn't have a lot to say. That evening our pastor came over to visit and pray with Kevin, and he had a different attitude about the whole thing. He used to get so nervous and scared and beg not to go, but this time he wasn't talking about it too much. He was sitting on the couch, and I saw two tears roll down his cheek and he said, "I wish I didn't have to go through this." It broke my heart to see him this way, but he recovered quickly and ate his dinner and talked with the pastor.

Later that night, things were just different—he had this far away look in his eyes, and he was so serene. I know that people have said that God gives us this peace right before we die, and we know that it is coming, and I wondered if this is what he was thinking. We went to bed, got up the next morning and drove to Atlanta to be admitted. He never complained the first time on the way down, he was just "different." We were admitted, and that night Kevin did not sleep very well. He was up most of the night even though they gave him something to make him sleep. The next morning, they gave him something to relax him. Nothing had ever worked before. He was always awake before going into the operating room, because he wanted to pray before going through the doors. We would always stay with him outside the doors while he prayed.

But this time, he was so drowsy that I could not understand what he was saying. They came to get him at 7 a.m., and we got to the operating room doors. He was so knocked out that I thought that there is no way he will be able to pray. So while everyone was gathered around his bed, I hugged him and told him I loved him, and then I left to go to the waiting room. I had *just gotten in the waiting room when a nurse came and told me that he wanted me to come back so he could pray. I went back, and he rose up the best he could, and he started praying, I couldn't understand a single word he said, but I know God did! I cried and cried for the longest.*

We all sat in the waiting room, and it was a very solemn time. We all tried not to worry about the surgery, but it was always lingering in the back of our minds as we talked together. We got updates throughout the day on the progress made. At around noon, a doctor came out to tell us that there was a problem. There was some excessive bleeding, and they thought it was scar tissue, but when they cut all the way through the sternum, they realized they had cut through the aorta. The aorta had attached itself to the sternum through the scar tissue. They had no way of knowing this with the X-rays and scans. So, they were going to have to repair the aorta before they could even start the corrective procedure. Also, they informed us that he had lost the blood supply to his brain and other organs when they cut through the aorta, and they didn't know exactly how long it had been. They only knew that he would be brain damaged to some extent if he survived the surgery.

Another negative for us to ponder...So, I went to the chapel, and I sat there crying and praying, and I remember I said, "God, I know you said you won't put anymore on us than we can handle, but I think I have reached my limit. I cannot stand the thought of Kevin coming out of this surgery not being Kevin anymore!" I continued to pray, and Warren and I went back to the waiting room. That afternoon was so long, and around 4 p.m. someone came and told us that they had finished the repair and were going to have to stop and finish the corrective surgery later.

So we waited and waited, and another report came. They had taken him off the heart- lung machine and were trying to put his blood back into his body, but everywhere they had made stitches the blood was seeping back out, it would not clot. They gave him so many transfusions trying to give the blood a chance to clot, but it never did.

At 5:08 p.m. on Oct. 2, 1991, the day before Warren's birthday, Kevin went to be with the Lord. I will never forget Dr. Williams face when he came around the corner. It was like one of those movies—you see the doctor come out, he has that look on his face, and you know that the person has died. I knew then that Kevin didn't make it. The worst had finally happened! It was like the world around me had stopped. I didn't know how to feel. I was numb. He talked to us and told us what had happened. Then he said that after we got home and everything was over, to make an appointment and come back down to see him, because he knew we would not remember what he had told us that day.

We saw Kevin one last time before we headed home, and I hated leaving him in Atlanta. The next few days were just a blur for us. We made the plans for the funeral, and we prayed a lot. More than 500 people signed the book at the funeral home, and many more that came and didn't get to sign the book at all.

Once it was all over and we were back home without Kevin, I had some time to reflect on things. We stayed busy, tried to keep occupied, but after thinking through the years, I do know that Kevin had made an impact on the lives of people we didn't even know. People would say, "I don't know what I would do if it were my child...I can't imagine what you are going through!" Well you do the things you have to do in this world, and if losing a child is one of those things, you just get through it. But you don't *get through it easily, and you don't get through it without God helping you! God has loaned us these children—they are not truly ours. They are his, and we have to trust him and know that he knows what is best. He has a purpose for all of us. After talking with all these people that told us of Kevin's impression on them, and how he had touched them, I know that God was honoring us in giving us a child like Kevin. I realized that we hadn't truly lost Kevin, because when his life ended here on earth, a brand new one began for him—one that was perfect and healthy—and we would see him again one day. You can't let the negative things overcome the positive things in this world because the positive is so much better than anything we can imagine.*

~Jan Coker

My Family Is Different

It is my realization that my family is different from others. We all love each other in spite of our faults. We get in arguments and disagree like everyone else, but it has never crossed my mind that we would not love each other tomorrow as much as we do today. I felt the same way about my husband. "All marriages have issues," they say. Well, mine was no exception. It wasn't until my husband of nearly 12 years told me that he wanted a divorce that I realized that we were in serious trouble. Sure, we had disagreements (among other issues), but I didn't know it was that bad until that day. I just thought things would eventually get better. They didn't, and we divorced in November.

Originally, I thought I would stay in the town where we lived. I had a good job, the girls went to a good school and our friends and church family were there. In the long run, I realized that was not going to be a good decision. My ex-husband already had a girlfriend, and the town was not big enough for both of us. I began to pray about it. For years I had asked my ex-husband to consider moving closer to my family. I had no family in our area, and I took this as my opportunity to move home. Then came the question of what is right for the girls. A very dear (and smart) friend of mine said, "The girls will be happy if their mother is happy. They are young and very outgoing. If you are considering doing this, it will be better sooner than later." Looking back at the series of events that have taken place, I can only come to the realization that God is definitely in control. Everything fell into place in succession.

I know that everyone deals with sadness in their own way. I generally tend to retreat. Our children, on the other hand, have not skipped a beat! God really does know what He is doing! My girls are so awesome. They are much stronger than their mother, or maybe I should say, "I am stronger because of their example." If it were not for them, I cannot tell you where I would be. Honestly, I don't think I would care. They have been such an inspiration to me, and I know without a doubt, they are Heaven sent. They are the reason I am making it through this. Have you heard that song, "God gave me you?" Most think about their significant others or their friends when they hear that song. I think about my girls.

People have asked me so many personal things, and it has been so hard to be honest when I don't know how I feel from minute to minute. I have tried so hard not to be bitter, but it a real struggle. I felt like I had been slapped in the face— sometimes I still just can't believe it. There have been days that I just wanted to crawl into a hole and sleep for a few months until things were "normal" again. But, I am very proud to say that I have not done that—not even for one day. Instead, I have come to the realization that even though I don't understand why this has happened to our family, God has a plan. And my job is to find out what that is. It is not easy—by any means—but I have found out so many things about myself.

Every day I pray that the day will be great, and I go ahead and thank God for my blessings, because I have so many of them. Through all of this, I have begun to realize just how much I have been blessed and I am more aware of it every day. If nothing else, this whole thing has reiterated to me to be thankful for my loved ones and thankful for my friends and family members. And, as hard as it is to admit, I have learned that I took some things for granted with my husband. If I marry again, I hope that I will not do that.

Today, I have no magic words. I only know how to put one foot in front of the other and hope for the best. I can do this because I am confident that God will take care of me. I am confident that there is a reason for my pain. I don't know what that reason is, and I may never know in this lifetime, but I know God's grace is real and He keeps his promises. So, I say YES to praying for those who disappoint you or rise up against you. Say YES to the challenges that life brings to your doorstep, even those you didn't ask for. Your challenges do not define you; how you respond to these challenges defines your character. And, say YES to faith over your feelings. This for me is much harder to do than to say, because I am an emotional person. It has helped me to talk about it with level-headed people.

You know, when I was younger, I thought that life was so simple—the golden rule and all that jazz. I was taught to treat others the way I wanted to be treated, and I feel like I have lived by that rule. The only problem is that not everyone lives by it. People don't always do the right thing. People don't always keep their promises, but God does. Sometimes it's easier for others to do what feels good at the moment. I say YES to loving them in spite of their behavior. Someone, like my girls, will learn from my example.

~Anonymous

Still See Mike

In 1975 I lost my husband to cancer. We both had said YES to God in accepting Him as our Savior earlier in our lives. After we married, we vowed to continue our walk with Him. Life was good. Saying YES was not a challenge. Saying YES was simple...then when Mike was 27, he was diagnosed with leukemia. It was terminal. God spoke to both of us. He was very clear when he asked, "Will you allow me to use this illness to reach others?"

What could I say? Mike had prayed the night before we left our home in Brunswick and said, "God use this illness for your glory." Our answer was YES. It was not an easy journey. I personally had no experience walking this particular road. We had two small children, and I found out two weeks after Mike's diagnosis I was three months pregnant with our third child. We went to Emory University for treatment. We had no money. We left the care of our two children with our family. We had no place for me to stay. We did not know anyone in Atlanta, and yet we knew answering YES to God meant He would provide. We witnessed miracles. We saw nurses and doctors say YES to God.

We had so many experiences that were unique to a young couple who answered YES.

I can still see Mike today as he would get off the elevator of the sixth floor at Emory Hospital with his suitcase in his hands ready to take his next chemo treatment, only to be stopped by nurses who said, "Mike, so and so wants to see you...so and so needs you.... Mike would put down his suitcase, pick up his rolling IV pole (he asked for one that was mobile) and with a positive spirit and a smile on his face, say YES.

Our journey together ended on January 5, 1975. I have often wondered where the road would have led had we answered differently. It really doesn't matter. I am grateful we traveled the road of YES. It was the road less traveled. One day I will share its curves, ruts and super highways.

~Betty Ryfun

A Gift of Grace to Someone Else

Sometimes, I think our answer YES may possibly be God's gift of grace to someone else. Maybe it's an answer we give to someone else, or maybe it's a YES from someone else when we need it most. Just a few nights ago, (it was a Monday...enough said), supper was late, bath time was late, bedtime was late. I started having this sinking feeling that I had all of these "hats," and not one of them could I wear and wear well. (It was a great pity/guilt party considering I was the one who was the inviter and only guest.) As I was helping my son, Harrison, get into bed, the thought crossed my mind just to skip prayer time altogether. Instead though, I crawled into bed beside him, listened as he said his, and then I offered up one that was, honestly just routine.

When I said, "Amen," Harrison said, "Wait...I have one more...Thanks for saying Mommy could be my Mommy."

When I picked my heart up off of the floor and kissed him goodnight, I silently prayed, "And may I always be the mommy he is thankful to have." Without actually saying it, Harrison gave me a YES answer that night. "YES...you are not just good enough for me...You are who I want!"

What if we have given someone a YES answer at just the right time, or (yikes)...what if we have neglected to give them that YES. As I have reflected on that night, I like to think that maybe that it wasn't just Harrison giving me affirmation. I like to think that it was God sending me a message too—his gift of grace in a way, through a child. Hmmm...Sounds familiar.

~Lindsay Gregg Peaster

Reflections

Where do you go to heal a broken life? That is the question we may sometimes ponder but don't always voice to the world around us. Can't we just go to the "start over place?" If we could just take an eraser and eliminate all of the spots where our life suddenly and unexpectedly colored outside the lines, then we would find peace.

There really isn't a "do-over place," as such. Many profess to have the one answer, but they don't.

The path to healing leads straight into your life. We must look fear in the eye. We must walk into the pain. We must face the naked truth of who we are, what happened, what we did or didn't do, what we did or didn't lose, and come to grips with the fact we are a broken person. Rather than deny or ignore the reality that has changed and will never be the same again, we try to learn. This is a painful truth to face on top of the hurt that has already occurred.

Only the Grace of God can make sense of and find a useful purpose for our brokenness. We may pursue magical words, instant answers, and quick fixes. But in the long run, they never work or provide the healing we desperately need at the core of our being—in our souls. We create our healthy place. This is where we learn to love ourselves and others with all of our being.

Rebirth

Prayer for Rebirth

Heavenly Father,

Going back to our beginnings has been a challenge. With honesty, we have had to look at our lives and pain that has been stored away in the "holy of holies." Now that you have entered into our sacred places, we are hearing another word—a distant one—that we have known for so very, very long. It is your word to us—grace, grace, God's grace. We are your adored and beloved children. You are well-pleased in us and who we are.

Our pain isn't the end of our story. It is just where the story took a turn in a different direction. Thank you, O' God, for a new beginning. You are working within us in ways we didn't realize. We have become so consumed with ourselves that we have left you outside. Help us hear your call to be the most authentic version of ourselves we can be. Help us to live with courage. Help us to live with joy, purpose, gratitude and humility. Help us to celebrate the gift of our lives. Thank you for leading us to the only home where our spirits can rest—at home with you.

In Christ's Name,

Amen

Cohesion

Merle Haggard accepted the prestigious award for lifetime achievement and "outstanding contribution to American culture" from the John F. Kennedy Center for the Performing Arts on December 4, 2010. During a television interview related to this award, he was asked how he would describe his music. His response was one word. He said, "Honest. I tried to be honest.[xxii]"

If you read any biography of his life, you will see a meandering journey of struggle, setback, success and achievement. His personal challenges have followed him. His success as a musician is reflected in having 39 number-one hits over a 30-year span. While I do not hold him up as a role model, I am intrigued by his answer—one word—*honesty*. What a simple idea: find one word or let one word find you and live it! How complicated do we try to make it?

The more I have thought about this brief response, the more I began to see that we all are given questions to answer by life and by circumstances beyond our control. One of mine has been, "How do you recover from the loss of a parent when you are young?" There have been many, many more that have come my way. Here are a few that have been life changers for me: How do you live by faith without being a religious fanatic? How do you reinvent your ministry when your beliefs are out of sync with the denomination? How do you recreate yourself when you believe you are being led into a different expression of ministry? How do you heal your life when it is broken?

The word I believe I have been given is *YES,* but it isn't just the word of affirmation to any and every request that may come my way. It is more than that. There are some dynamics to it. My YES for life is formed where my life, God's presence, and human need merge into a cohesive source of energy, passion and direction. My YES has a voice, and it is mine. I have been given a voice to speak to and for the discouraged, struggling and inconsistent followers of Christ. My mission is to offer encouragement and hope to the ones who want to give up or have grown weary of trying. YES becomes a word to speak, a voice to share, and a life to be lived.

This gives me a sense of cohesion. My life fits together in ways I never imagined. The pain and disappointments become a source of healing and hope. There is cohesion, unity and wholeness. The puzzle makes sense even if all of the pieces don't fit together the way that I think that they should.

When we get to the point that we can hear our question, then we are walking down the path where we will discover our word. The world needs us to find it. There are people who hunger to hear solutions to life's biggest problems, but they don't want to hear from the experts or self-appointed gurus. They want to hear the voice of a fellow pilgrim who can say, "I have walked that road, and you can make it through." They don't want a quick fix, a superficial answer, or a religious platitude. They want the truth—the one that comes from deep within the soul of someone who has known what it is like to walk through the darkness and see the light on the other side.

The world is waiting to hear *your* word. They will listen for *your* voice. They will watch *your* life. There are so many who need it—now!

A Word Emerges

Word

Your life is a word. In fact, our lives are many words merging together to create our word to the world. I don't think we can hear our word until we let some other ones merge into the essence of you are. These are critical to understanding our past, present, and future.

While reading "The Signature of Jesus," written by Brennan Manning, I came across the statement: "...we are all called, to listen attentively to God's first word to us. This word is the gift of ourselves to ourselves – our existence, our nature, our personal history, our uniqueness, our identity. All that we have and are is one of the unique and never to be repeated ways God has chosen to express himself in space and time."[xxiii] I couldn't shake the words from my spirit. I began to see myself in a different way. I realized that I am one of God's words being expressed into this world in which I live.

My life is a word. It is God's word of life being created, formed and shaped by every experience, relationship and event. I am a gift to me. I am a gift to the world. These are difficult ones to hear because we look at ourselves and see imperfections, mistakes or faults. While these "big chunks of brokenness" are ever with us, there is another truth that permeates every cell of physical, emotional and spiritual being—we are loved by the God of this universe.

Brokenness

Your life is broken. I want to believe that God loves me and that I am a word he wants to speak, but I see an inconsistent person who often struggles, stumbles and falls. In the cracks of brokenness, there is the "glue" of God's love. What holds me together is a love I cannot see, touch, hold, create, earn or influence. I can't make God love me more by being good, noble, kind or considerate. I cannot make God love me less by being rude, selfish, critical or self-centered. God love's because it his nature to do so.

All Christians know this truth, but most Christians haven't experienced the fullness of it. Why would I make this statement? I see so many who profess faith who still have trouble accepting who they are as a person, their experiences and their dreams. I found these words in the book, "The Furious Longing of God." "Every Christian knows God loves him or her—it is a tenant of faith—more than experience of the heart. Until it gets into your heart, it remains information. Once it gets into your heart, it becomes transformation."[xxiv]

Our brokenness becomes transformed by the love of God. It is not removed. The pain still hurts. The scars remain. The residue of on-going confusion will continue. The brokenness is the "workshop for God's grace" to begin to mend, mold and change who we are and who we will become as a result of the broken places.

Waiting

Your life is waiting.

You are waiting to be the alive, vibrant and engaging person you believe you were created and are being called to be. So, what is the problem? Are you waiting on someone to give you permission to be that person? Who do you need to give you permission? Is it a parent, spouse, child, neighbor, friend? Are you waiting on the right situation to appear? Are you waiting on someone from the past to walk up and say, "I am sorry?" Are you waiting on your ex-spouse to drive by and say, "I was wrong?"

As long as we wait, we are stuck. Someone or something else holds control over our lives. We may want to go back to the past or fast forward to the future, but our life has hit the "pause button" and action has stopped.

I think waiting serves a good purpose if it is healthy. You can't start a business without a plan. You can't start a family without some thought or strategy. We need to let things sit and cook for awhile until the timing is right. That is a good use of waiting to me. When we pause because of fear, uncertainty or doubt, I don't think that is as healthy. We are allowing something within to make us slow down or even stop what might be a wonderful new direction or purpose.

Your word will never be spoken as long as you are waiting. It can be formed, shaped, and molded, and these are good developments. It will be spoken when your life is ready.

YES

I believe my word is *YES*. I didn't discover it as much as it discovered me. I remember always having an interest in helping people overcome obstacles. I like to offer encouragement whether that is giving someone a call or offering a reminder. I knew it was one I wanted to hear when I was young. Can I go play? Like any child, I only wanted to hear the affirmative. Can I get this toy? You guessed it—I wanted to hear YES.

I didn't realize it was my word for a long time. Only, when I was talking with a friend and my wife did the question surface, "How Can I Live YES in a NO World?" Then I knew why that question held my attention.

It is more than three letters. It contains a lifetime of meaning for me. It is the affirmation that I am a person of worth and value. It is agreement with the reality I face. It is being open to the full range of life experience. It is, at the deepest level, a word that I must speak to myself, God and the world. YES is my definition of life and how I choose to live it under the guidance of God's spirit.

You have a word. Yours will not be the same as mine. It shouldn't be. Your life, circumstances, gifts, talents, interests, hopes and dreams are unique to you.

YES is my fingerprint in the world. Your word is ready to emerge in you.

Living in the Land of YES

I love the word *YES*. When you live with YES, you are open, receptive and available. Each moment comes filled with curiosity, adventure, openness and anticipation. Everyday seconds turn into exciting minutes when we receive the gift of each one.

You don't shut down or close yourself off. You don't run away or hide. You are present, alive, alert and aware of what is taking place. YES becomes your open door to all of what life is bringing your way and all that comes with it.

NO

I love the word *NO*. It is a beautiful thought and a powerful action. When you say NO, you end movement, reaction, exchange and relationship. It protects you from harm, abuse and misunderstanding. It ends; it draws to a close; it creates a boundary—If you assign it the role, responsibility and power you want it to utilize then it becomes the protector of what is most valuable to you.

If NO becomes an attitude toward life, it can become a very negative force and hold us back. Listen to some of these expressions and see if they ever creep into our thoughts:

- I want him to change his behavior.
- I want her to stop doing that.

- I don't want this to happen.
- I want to feel differently about this situation.
- She shouldn't be doing that.
- My parents should have loved me.
- My husband should support me.
- My wife should encourage me.

Can you feel the NO in each one? There is a limit. You can sense the desire to back someone or "state of being" into a corner. Unfortunately, nothing changes. Reality stays the same. An old saying goes, "That which you resist persists." Something odd takes place when we resist reality—it gives strength to the experience or person you wish would disappear.

A Discerning YES

Living with YES does not make you a pushover, doormat, or weak person. Your YES discerns what you need to do. When you see life as it is, your blinders are removed. You see people and situations for what they are. You are being honest with yourself about what is in front of you. It becomes easier to take action because you know exactly what you are dealing with. You are making a choice on how to respond. It is a freeing experience to know that you have the power to decide what you will think, feel and do. It is your one word of judgment.

Suppose you make plans to meet a friend for dinner. He is always late. You arrive on time. He doesn't. You sit and wait...Before long, you begin to feel frustrated. Your mind starts to dwell on the negative—"He is always late; I am always on time; I shouldn't have set this up." The tape plays over and over. Now, stop the tape. All of this is filled with NO. This is resistance. Nothing is being changed except the emotional climate within you.

Now, say YES to the moment. Accept the YES that is in front of you—your friend is late, you are getting uptight and you are frustrated. You can accept the fact your friend is late and turn it into a different experience. Stop worrying about something you cannot control. Be open, receptive and available to what is around you. Listen to the conversations at other tables. Notice the setting and people. Look for ways to bring joy to the moment. Or, you can call your friend and remind him you only have ten minutes before you must leave. Learn to appreciate him for who he is. He isn't being late to frustrate you. He is being late because it is a habit he has developed.

You have the freedom and power to change. You can choose to look at the event with a different point of view and interpret it in a way that limits the NO or negative energy.

Living with YES

- YES is the gift of my life to me.

- YES is embracing the gift with all of the joy and all of the sadness that may come with it.

- YES is love, grace and healing.

- YES is recreating life with the pieces I have to work with.

- YES is my deepest response to the God of this universe and all that I have been allowed to experience.

- YES is my reply to life.

- YES is embracing my entire journey and seeing the beauty in each "turn in the road." For YES is grace. As Brennan Manning suggests, "To live by grace means to acknowledge my whole life story, the light side and the dark."[xxv]

Unique

One of the great temptations you will face is choosing between being an authentic self and being a fake, pretender, or impostor. On the surface, it appears to be an easy answer. No one really sets out to be artificial or counterfeit, but we sometimes ease into it as a protection device. It is easier and simpler to act like we are okay or be someone else rather than let family and friends know how we really feel. This prevents us from having to walk into the pain. We can keep hurt, disappointment and emotions boxed up in a package that we can keep stored away in the closet of our heart somewhere.

The beauty of YES calls you to gather up all of your taped up boxes of stuff, open them up, and release the negative energy that has been crammed into some old memories you no longer need. The expiration date for them being of any value to you has long passed. The day your mother didn't take you shopping when you were 10 isn't a useful memory when you are 40. The weekend the in crowd from school didn't invite you to go to the beach when you were in high school is long past being useful for you. There comes a time in every situation that you let go of the right or privilege to hurt.

Open

The authenticity of YES calls you to be open, honest and transparent. It invites you to come out in the open and let your real self be present. You can relax in the embrace of love, acceptance and forgiveness. For many, these thoughts are threatening and filled with fear.

Being open puts you in a position to experience the depth, width and height of all that life has to offer. You embrace love knowing that hate is always a possibility. You enter relationships knowing they may end. You give but also must learn to take. You receive life as it is with what is taking place. You accept the "gift of now" without trying to judge or change it.

Honesty requires truthfulness with yourself and others. Here is an idea to consider. If you don't practice being honest, what happens? The obvious answer is that you become dishonest. Other options might be that you hide, pretend or fake—none of these sound very healthy because they aren't. They prolong painful memories and artificial approaches to life. You spend more energy trying to avoid reality than actually dealing with it.

Transparency must be learned. Few people have the innate ability to share what they truly feel without hesitation. Like any new skill, confidence comes with practice. Being open and honest leads to a desire to share what you see, feel, like or dislike without any thought of rejection. This frees you to embrace all of your emotions.

And you learn to trust again. You find confidence within yourself you didn't know you possessed. You learn to discern what is reliable, within your control, and what is not. You invest yourself more carefully but with a deeper commitment.

Alive

There is a zest, vitality and passion to being your authentic, open and receptive self. You are present to your life and moments. You are available and accessible. Being alive is a gift to be cherished. The opportunity to engage and interact gives purpose. It means discovering the ability to make a difference and not just make a point.

Being alive means you approach each moment as though it is the first time you ever went barefoot in the spring. Your senses are on high alert. You feel the tingle of fresh grass when you see a sunrise. You smell the first whiff of honeysuckle blooms in every conversation. You delight at the experience of being able to see, hear and taste what the next day or person may bring.

Balance

Can you love too much? Well, yes you can if you let your concern ignore boundaries and try to do too much for the other person that they could do for themselves. Can you tell the truth too much? If you try to use honesty to help others see reality that is healthy. If you use it to brutalize and beat down by just telling it like you see it that may not be an effective way to relate. Balance is the solution.

A healthy life, a YES life, seeks balance. There is a need to keep people, events, relationships and needs in perspective. You do care, but you respect boundaries and individual space. You do tell the truth, but you utilize it as a way to relate to reality and people in a productive way. You never compromise your integrity, but you don't act like a religious fanatic to make a point.

A balanced life strives for a healthy approach.

Change

You live from your center where you know you are loved, forgiven and whole. At your core, you know what you have experienced and accept the past just for what it is— preparation for being the person you are now. You look back at earlier mistakes and hurts with a non-judgmental approach. You can revisit old conversations and hear new truths you had missed.

You have peace. Because old wounds have healed and tough scars formed in their place, you don't have to pretend or put on your happy face. The calm of acceptance and forgiveness surrounds you. You can be authentic. No pretense or pretending. No mask or masquerade. You can be who you are. This means YES becomes a very unique experience.

You will have to do the work in your own life to discover the path YES will lead you to take, but when you do, you have begun the second journey of life. Where all the pieces from the first journey have been re-examined, kept or thrown away, and a new path emerges that leads to an undiscovered future—one that will be revealed as you trust the leadership of God's spirit, listen for the still small voice, and forge into the promise of another tomorrow.

Tapping into a Deeper Source

When I was young, our family relied upon three sources of water for our livelihood—a spring, a creek and a well. When the old well that had provided water to our home was no longer functional, an alternative source was needed. A city or county supply didn't exist where we lived. The option of digging a new well was pursued but abandoned for reasons I can't remember.

Getting water out of a free-flowing creek for family consumption wouldn't work due to contamination. There was a small one near our house that would have been available. As children, we played in it often with great imagination. At the time, I thought it was large, but in reality it was only about 4 to 5 feet across. One day a cousin and I hatched a plan to dam up the creek and divert the water to a farm pond. It was a nice-size pond where we could catch an occasional bass, catfish or blue gill, and that was our motivation. Our thinking was: direct the water from the creek to the pond, the pond gets deeper, and there will be more fish. It was a plan... and it worked. We placed large boulders and small logs in the water at a critical point, and the flow moved from the creek through a small ditch to the pond. Over the next couple of days, the water level in the pond increased dramatically—that is until my uncle began to wonder why there wasn't any water flowing into the fields where he had planted corn. That was the end of the dam.

A natural spring was found, a pipe line was dug, and fresh water flowed again. It was cool, clear and sweet. It became a natural resource for several nearby homes as well.

Near our home there were many artesian springs. One located by the highway approximately two miles east of where we lived had become a popular stopping place for travelers. Many would stop, fill up a container, or drink right out of the strong flow of water that poured from a pipe placed in the lip of the opening. It was known as *Godsey's Spring* because Reverend Godsey owned the land. Any time of day or night you stopped, the water pressure was always the same—a gushing spout.

These images serve as a wonderful example of the varied ways we try to nourish our lives.

> A Well: A man-made effort to find something that will quench the thirst.
> A Creek: A natural flowing resource that moves along the surface of the earth but prone to contamination as well as drying up or being flooded.
> A Spring: A deep bubbling source of clear, clean and naturally purified water.

Everyone looks for nourishment in life. We just take different approaches. One person may try to "dig their own well" so they make every effort to create, form and shape something that satisfies based upon their desires and needs. They dig deep hoping to "strike it rich" and find the source for happiness, peace, or contentment.

Another person may pursue that which "flows along the surface" trying to find a solution that can be quickly reached. Though it can be easily accessed it is open to pollution, drought and flooding. There isn't any consistency to it.

Then there is a need to connect to the deepest sources of flow where the current bubbles, gushes and pours out to nurture thirsty spirits. You don't always know where to find it or gain access to it.

To me, this last one is an image for YES. It is getting reconnected to your past in a way that brings healing; connecting to God in quiet and reflective practices that feed your walk of faith; and celebrating the gift of your life in a way that keeps you present, receptive and available to participate in each moment. Energy and vitality flow freely from the deep places of God's presence. Because you are loved, healed and forgiven, his grace flows through every thought, word and action. You become a channel for the current of his spirit to flow through you.

For me, I have struggled to define YES. At first, I approached it as a simple response that could be used to answer a question. Over time, the definition has evolved and transformed. I now see it as our ultimate response to the universe. It is what I am being asked to do in reply to the detours, roadblocks, or construction zones that I encounter on my journey through this place.

For me, YES invites me to:

- Accept my life as a gift from God to be loved, embraced, cherished and nurtured.

- Affirm my connection to God, drawing upon faith, hope and love as positive sources of power in shaping my life as I seek to practice a simple faith of trust and service.

- Face reality head on as I walk through adversity and look at it as an opportunity to learn and grow in God's strength, finding a way through the dark times with courage, honesty and transparency.

- Accept God's grace for the broken places, seeing my weakness as a point where God can give me strength as his grace shines through the shattered pieces.

- Embrace the healing of my soul as an on-going journey of forgiveness, acceptance, affirmation, reconciliation and renewal.

- Utilize healthy resources for spiritual, emotional and physical well-being.

- Recreate my life as I hear God's voice calling me to live YES again after each setback and for each new stage in my journey.

- Hold close mindful moments of grace with gratitude as I seek his presence in the routine of everyday life, casual conversations, and the ordinary experience of being alive.

- Create a community of YES faith that offers encouragement and hope for those who desire healing, completion and wholeness.

This is YES to me. These thoughts are fluid and ever-changing. I hope that they will never become rigid commands to be followed as much as reflections to be adjusted with each new breeze of the Spirit in this ever changing adventure.

Celebrating the New House

The house that was home to me as a child was literally an "old house." There was no central heat or air conditioning—only a coal stove and open windows. There was no indoor plumbing—only an outhouse and a well. There were only three rooms.

My dad, with help from family and friends, built a new house. It was much larger than the old one with two bedrooms, living room, dining room, kitchen and bath. There was a gas heater to keep us warm. It was constructed carefully and furnished with love.

Like all homes, it had limitations. Life stopped by and cancer paid an untimely visit. My dad didn't get to enjoy the labor of his hands for very long. His life changed... and so did mine.

Since then, I have spent a lot of time looking for home. I think most of us do. It is a never-ending search for the feeling of safety and security from the storms. We want a place where we will be held in a mother's loving arms, protected by a father's care, and cherished by a grandparent's adoration. Deep down we want to be at home with ourselves and our lives. We want peace and contentment. We want our lives to be healed and whole.

Unfortunately, we don't always find our resting place. We keep looking and spend impatient night's pacing the floor longing for a rest that will satisfy the deep needs of the spirit. Guy Sayles shares a timely insight from Dorothy Day's autobiography, "The Long Loneliness," where she reveals she was able to get through the tough times by remembering some words from St. Teresa of Avila: "Life is a night spent in an uncomfortable inn."[xxvi]

This doesn't mean we are all condemned to live out our existence in a cheap motel where the pillows are lumpy, mattresses squeaky and walls thin. Instead, it is a reminder that this world is not our destination. We are only passing through for a little while. Later in his own words, Guy states, "Don't be surprised when life in the here-and-now leaves you feeling restless, anxious, helpless and out of touch. You weren't made for life under these conditions. So, don't be surprised, but don't despair either, because there is a place where your tired spirit will find rest and your anxious heart will find perfect peace. There is a home for you—the home you have yearned for all of your life. That home is not exactly a place; it is a person. Your home is with Jesus."[xxvii]

In the Gospel of John, on the night before his death, Jesus gathered friends and family together for final words of instruction on what would soon occur. Their world was about to be turned upside down—they would plummet to the depths of despair only to be launched to the heights of true joy. The promise Jesus made that night was about home. [1] "Do not let your hearts be troubled. You believe in God; believe also in me. [2] My Father's house has many rooms; if that were not so, would I have told you that I am going there to prepare a place for you? [3] And if I go and prepare a place for you, I will come back and take you to be with me that you also may be where I am." (John 14: 1-3).

The promise is for them and for us: a home with God, a place where joy grows, because sadness has ended; a place where lives are whole, because hurts have been healed; a home where laughter echoes in every room, because weeping is no more. There is a home that is with God. There is a place we all long to find—not a bad night's sleep in a lousy motel but a resting place where there is joy and happiness, peace and contentment, and rest and renewal.

I have moved many times since the days in the "old house." I have lived in a variety of structures from a mobile home to apartments to a partially furnished basement to large homes. I have discovered that contentment isn't found in a building. It is found in your heart. Home is within you. Home is within me. Until I create my sense of home with my life and journey, I will never find a resting place. But once I do—there is much joy and celebration in knowing I am loved beyond anything I can understand, forgiven beyond any mean deed I can commit, and I am cherished by the God of this universe as one of his special children.

I was reminded of how much we all long for this resting place when my friend Carol Mathias shared the concept of this book with some of her friends at a hair salon. As she described the idea of YES, people around her began to ask questions. Some stopped what they were doing and walked closer so that they could hear better. She then told them the story of "He will hear enough NO in his life. I wanted him to hear YES." As she did, everyone in the business stopped, stylists walked over, clients got up from under the dryers and stood around. I don't think it was just the story. I don't think it is just the concept of the book. I think it is a need that we all experience at a very deep level.

We want to find YES. We want to live YES. It is my privilege to say to you, "Welcome home my child. It is time for you to rest a little while—live YES with joy, excitement, vitality, purpose and intent. You are home now."

Sacred Stories

Putting a Face to It

My husband, Rick, and I were invited to lead music for an HIV/AIDS Healing Retreat. It was held at Kanuga Episcopal Conference Center near Hendersonville, NC. We were excited yet uncertain at the same time. We knew how to lead the music. We were not as confident in being able to use music to build a connection with those in attendance.

The retreat was designed for anyone who had been affected by AIDS. This included those who were victims, family members, partners or friends. Diversity didn't end there. Every layer of society was present as well in different races, economic resources, and social setting. It didn't seem to matter that who sat where or what your role in life was. All who had been impacted by AIDS in some way had come together for this weekend because they were hurting and needed to be there.

We experienced a lot of apprehension around how to relate to so much diversity. The music did it for us. That and God's Spirit. After our first session, Mary, a 90-year-old African American mother who had lost her son to AIDS, walked up to tell us how much she enjoyed the music. Her affirmation gave us the confidence to trust our instincts in leading the music throughout the weekend. She helped us find the freedom and to let go of our fear. Her "yes" had the power to change the way we worked with others and to allow God to work through us.

The featured speaker had talked of "putting a face" on HIV/AIDS. It was a challenge we all felt and desired to do. This lovely, 90 year old mother confided that she had never told people in her community that her son had died of AIDS. She was embarrassed and ashamed. She was a college professor and a church choir director. How could HER son die of AIDS?

At the end of the closing service on the last day as people began to leave, she went up to the piano and began to play. It was a piece she had written for her son. She told Rick and I that she planned to go back to her community; to "put HIS face" on HIV/AIDS. She was ashamed that she had kept it a secret. She no longer feared sharing her pain and through it helping others to heal.

It was a wonderful retreat and great weekend. Rick and I were deeply touched by the whole experience. This mother's honesty and transparency were so genuine. Hearing her say YES to the loss of her son but allowing her hurt to become transformed into action, has changed us.

~*Angee Knight McKee*

Getting My Life Back

In January 2008, I was arrested and charged with child molestation. I spent 19 months away from home, isolated from my wife and two daughters, facing possible life in prison, fighting to prove my innocence and save my family. How this happened, what I did about it, and the way this experience has shaped my life will be with me forever. Telling the story is the best way I know to portray my strengths, abilities and weaknesses in hopes that others might find encouragement to stay strong in times of adversity.

The ordeal began when I fell asleep in my seven-year-old daughter's bed. In the middle of the night, she shook me awake, and I was startled to find I had touched her during sleep. Since both of our children were very young, there wasn't anything odd *about one of the kids sleeping with us sometimes, or us with them.*

Although the act was unintentional, my wife and I were heartbroken it happened. And although our daughter seemed fine, we worried that, if we didn't seek professional help for her, one day she might not be. Despite the risks, I consulted a family counselor and voluntarily reported the incident to the Department of Family and Children Services ("DFCS") in our state.

Everyone initially agreed this was a tragic accident. But after our daughter was interviewed, DFCS told us she reported things that were inconsistent with my account of the incident: horrible things I couldn't believe and ones she had never suggested before. We discovered later that she didn't actually say these things. Instead, the interview was contaminated with errors, and she was largely misunderstood, ignored, and misrepresented. Nevertheless, the authorities inferred the worst. I was precluded from all contact with my children, and subsequently arrested.

When I bonded out of jail, I found a great attorney and began working with him and his team to prove that whatever happened that night happened while I was asleep and incapable of intent. We compiled a mass of supporting evidence, including a polygraph test, psychosexual evaluation, medical diagnosis of a related sleep disorder, support from the DFCS-appointed therapist, and expert criticism of my daughter's interview. We took it all to the district attorney, but it didn't help. I finally conceded that the only chance for an acceptable outcome was to take it to a jury.

At trial, my daughter was among the state's first witnesses. When she walked into court and took the stand, it was the first time we'd seen each other in more than a year and a half. The prosecutor asked her if she knew why she was there. "To get my daddy back," she said. After a week of hearing arguments and less than two hours of deliberation, the jury acquitted me of all charges.

Every day since then has been a process of picking up the pieces and healing my family. The emotional struggles we endured, and the "life lessons" that continue to materialize for me, are too many to name. Ultimately, I just learned how to survive. We all did. I also learned that I needed to be a lawyer. It's not because I'm on a mission to right a wrong that's been done to me. Although some people got it all wrong, I believe they only did what they felt was right. And it's not because I think the legal system is so broken that I need to try to fix it. Indeed, it worked for me in the end, perhaps exactly the way it was meant to. Rather, I am compelled to enter the profession because my experience ignited a profound interest in the law, because I discovered I had an aptitude for it and because I think I have something important and valuable to share.

I have to admit, there were many times I thought of saying NO. Thoughts of suicide and fleeing the country occurred to me. And at one point, just before the trial, some 18 months into the ordeal, I thought of giving up by entering a plea. Although I knew I had the truth on my side and the best counsel available, I was so afraid of being found guilty, of receiving a mandatory minimum sentence of 25 to life, that I decided it might be preferable to plead to something and serve some time if I knew there would be an end to it, at which point I could return to my family and start over. Certainty and finality, it seemed, was better, and perhaps more responsible, than taking my chances with a jury.

Cast in this light, I guess, in a way, you could say that even that was a form of saying YES—yes to the possibility of a future life for me, and yes to the possibility that my wife and our girls would have a husband and father again—where the possibility for such in the alternative scenario was very uncertain. It was one of the many tough decisions I had to make. I thank God that the prosecution's offer was unacceptable, and truly left me "no choice" but to proceed to trial. Otherwise, I probably would be in prison right now. Of course, this "no choice," as I describe it, was a choice. I didn't have to go through with it. Even up to the last day of the trial, while the jury was still out, I had other options— which I've already mentioned—than to wait for a verdict. But I didn't exercise them, perhaps because all of them were resounding NOs. When the trial was over, my lead attorney, who had become like a father to me, told me how proud he was that I had decided to go the distance, how few had the courage to do so, how several of his clients had committed suicide, and many had otherwise given up.

My faith did change. During my "dark night of the soul," I feel like I found God; although intermittently, I would lose Him again and wonder where He went. I read "Man's Search for Meaning," "When Bad Things Happen to Good People," "Siddhartha," "The Heart of Christianity;" I listened to Wayne Dyer's book, "Power of Intention" repeatedly; I prayed the Serenity Prayer. And all of this helped me understand how to have a relationship with God (or the Divine, or a Higher Power, or whatever you want to call it, all of which, to me, became the same), how to trust Him, how to surrender, how to live the words, "Thy will be done." I never had that before. And, as I've said, I lost it intermittently along the way, and it continues to come and go, now. But having found it once, I know how to find it again.

But perhaps my greatest discovery was the power of the love and compassion of others, which is what, more than anything else, gave me the strength to survive. Hearing YES from others sustained me and helped me say YES to faith, to my circumstances, to my fate. I witnessed the ability to forgive, and experienced the struggle to allow oneself to be forgiven. I felt our collective, utter brokenness, and recognized our need for compassion, forgiveness, and love. I considered the degree to which human love reflects (or is) Divine love. I concluded that *sharing that love, showing that compassion is perhaps our very reason for being.*

Many of the YES moments have come in the aftermath of our ordeal, after the trial, and after I returned home. Because we were separated from each other for so long, my wife and I did much of our healing independently. We each accepted and faced our woundedness in different ways. I remain convinced that this was as it should have been: heal yourself before you attempt to heal others—put the oxygen mask on yourself before attempting to assist others with theirs. Still, when we were reunited, there was a lot of work left to done—and still is. But our ultimate YES has been to each other, to rebuilding our family, and to turning an experience that was so bad into some good. That's part of what led me to law school, and what has led my wife and our girls to support me in and sacrifice for this journey.

Years ago, Steve Jobs delivered the commencement address at a Stanford University graduation. In that speech, he talked about, among other things, how the dots of his life, the seemingly unrelated experiences he had accumulated, connected in ways he never could have expected, to create the life and work he ended up with. I try to trust that, as Jobs said, my "dots will somehow connect to my future." I try to trust that I am, right now, where I was intended to be, doing what I was intended to be doing—and that the same will be true tomorrow. I was led to law school by a traumatic life experience. If I could go back and scratch out that part of my life, I certainly would, because it was (and, in many ways, continues to be) too painful to want to relive, and because it caused the people I love the most as much pain as it did me. However, it is now as much a part of me as my heart. I wouldn't be the person I am without it, and I wouldn't be on the path I'm on—to wherever I'm going—if I had taken a different turn.

"It is what it is," became my mantra throughout the ordeal. It was where I was and, for reasons I couldn't explain, but came to accept (through faith in a higher power, a larger plan, an unknowable but comforting purpose/intention), was where I

was meant to be. Now, "connecting the dots," I know I wouldn't be in law school without it. And I know the journey isn't nearly over—that merely becoming a lawyer is not the end of it, the reason for it. There will be other dots to connect somewhere down the road, other "reasons" I experienced what I did. And there will be dots for others who shared the experience with me, because it was not mine, alone.
~**Anonymous**

Opening New Doors with Chappy

The immortal work of Mary Stevenson's 1936 poem, "Footprints in the Sand," relates how God carries us during difficult times, and one set of footprints is proof of His presence during those times. I was in dire need of the same proof of footprints. The big ball of grief I carried around needed acknowledging. Bone tired from fighting back tears and swallowing the lump in my throat, I attempted to hold it together until I got to the beach. The upcoming trip would give me the time and place to let go of the emotions that had built up since June 15. I could scream into the crashing waves, and hopefully the hot wind would dry my tears. The only witnesses to my breakdown would be the footprints left by shell seekers, fiddler crabs and joggers. If they could talk, what would they say? "Yes, I've been here with my bike...Yes, I walked with my dog...Yes, I ran in my shoes...Yes, the turtles nested here." It was a perfect plan for a dignified nervous breakdown, right?

The previous couple of years had been a very exciting time for our family. My daughter, Rosemary, married Palmer, the man of her dreams, in a storybook perfect wedding and became pregnant with their first child. When things go well, most of us like to think that we can predict, control and manage what is around the next bend. We focus on the end product, and hurry through the journey. The process of pregnancy is a commercialized tradition of baby showers, gift registries, name selections, and nursery design plans. We were not immune to the sirens of Toys r' Us, Baby Depot, and all adorable little things in blue. It is hard to resist the excitement of the anticipated arrival and family celebration of YES, he is here. All the milestones of pregnancy, obstetrical visits, and healthy indicators amplified our encouragement for a healthy baby, Charles Chapman Bailey due on June 15. On that day, in an instant, our YES world turned to NO.

Delivery day began with the medical traditions common to most families of expectant parents. Rosemary and Palmer arrived early and settled into the labor and delivery suite, prepped for an induction and the waves of contractions to push our "bundle of joy" out into the world. The extended family and a few close friends gathered and bonded over stories, vending machine snacks and nervous laughter. The wait got longer than was comfortable while we glanced at the time, texted, and worried about the delays. The decision was quickly made at the end of a long day of highs and lows, to perform an emergency C-section. The YES mood began to dwindle, and the energy sank into one of guarded concern.

In the minutes following his birth, my life was no longer separated into personal and professional domains. I ceased to be a mother, grandmother, therapist or friend. I had one life now, and my well-planned worlds of YES and NO were no longer compartmentalized. Acceptance is one big hairy, messy, frustrating YES.

The body language and grim faces of nurses and pediatricians revealed a series of issues with his breathing, ability to regulate vital body systems and a serious congenital heart defect known as tetralogy of fallot, which occurs in five out of every 10,000 babies. The real culprit in all these minute-by-minute changes was one extra little chromosome, Trisomy 21, which altered the genetic and developmental makeup of our precious new grandson. What I know now is that disability is

291

just ability in disguise. But what I experienced in that moment was the echo of NO, this can't be happening—shattering the world as I wanted and imagined it would be for my children and grandson.

The NO moments of life hijack us into fits of anger, seeking someone to blame, or embarrassment at our own prejudice, shame and vulnerability. As the doctor sat on the edge of Rosemary's bed and filled her in on the grave situation, I leaned against the wall in order to keep my knees from buckling and my legs from collapsing beneath me. I scanned the eerie silence and noticed the strange grey look of shock on the faces of people in her hospital room. Some silently sobbed, others buried their face in their hands, and jaws dropped in the wave of denial. I remembered that true panic needs three ingredients to take hold of a person: (1) the sensation that one is possibly trapped; (2) everyone around you is feeling the same; (3) and nothing can be done to rescue you. All three components were present in that room. I watched in agony as my daughter, a pediatric nurse herself, struggling to wake up from the black hole of anesthesia, listened and forced out her only statement: "Well, it will take me a few minutes to wrap my head around all this." In that instant, I watched YES and NO merge into unconditional love for my child, and for her child—the precious gift who would change life as we know it.

What do the concepts of footprints, YES and NO have in common here? First, learning how to trust your ability to let go of YES and NO is a life lesson when your daughter gives birth to a son with medical challenges and uncharted developmental delays. Second, his special footprint is the significant marker for the diagnosis of Down syndrome and the most recognizable logo of Down's organizations. Finally, his birth raises the standards for living a YES life and being grateful for the confusion of the NO messages we receive. I know that my footprints on my path of dreams and hopes are not valuable unless they are based on

God-given steps. Chapman's extra chromosome freed me from those useless things that needed pruning from my life.

You do not become conscious of experiencing the messages from footprints or the quality of your YES and NO moments by talking about them—no more than shopping for baby clothes makes you prepared for the arrival of an infant. You start living them in the mindfulness of the moment, enjoying the journey, waiting for ordinary and the miracles to show up. The greatest breakthrough has been what God has put in my heart in the form of patience, faith and strength. Our lives now focus on the gift of raising a child who happens to have Down syndrome, and not a "Down syndrome" baby. Perfect love lights a candle in the darkness of frightening circumstances.

After the shock of learning you have a child with special needs, most families wonder if they are prepared for what they are about to face. Chapman had a frightening surgery at 2 weeks to correct a duodenal obstruction, and will be facing major heart surgery by age 6 months. He has created for us a comfort level with uncertainty and a new life appreciation and perspective that I've longed for, but was too cowardly to embrace on my own. He has taught us to surrender to love in dimensions that few rarely experience and he has shown the best and worst of our deep well of strength.

For me, personally, he has delivered me from a world of needing YES in the form of perfection and control. I am not special, saintly, or strong. I learned that I could be sloppy, sad, self-absorbed, and at peace with all of it. This is quite a relief when we struggle to live in a culture that puts a premium on perfection, self-sufficiency and willful independence.

It is a whole new world, and the end of life, as we knew it. God is in control, and in His footprint we will be given the answer to how to walk, what to give up, when to surrender, and the joy of just being in love with His wonderful YES to life creation— Charles Chapman Bailey, our precious "Chappy."
~**Carol Chapman Mathias**

Jane Moss: Living YES in the NO World of Cancer

This NO world has a way of discouraging people. I would like to tell you about how my wife, Jane, chose to live a YES life in the midst of this NO world. When Jane and I first knew we were going to be parents, we made a decision that if we were able to raise our children on one income, we would. God blessed us by opening doors that allowed us to raise our children on one income. This allowed Jane to work and volunteer in the schools where our children attended, and later she began serving as a substitute teacher.

Once our children were in high school and college, Jane was hired in a small town primary school as a paraprofessional teacher's assistant working with Special Needs children. Her best days were when she came home energized because one of her kids had learned a new skill or comprehended a new book. Yet, it was those skills that her kids struggled with that invigorated Jane to seek solutions. She would spend hours going from book to book, and website to website, seeking new ideas on how to help her kids triumph over that skill that they struggled with. She loved these kids, and God opened the doors that allowed her to return to school to get her teaching degree in Education for Special Needs Children and receive her Teaching Certificate in the State of Georgia. Thus Jane began a career that she loved, helping children conquer new learning skills that would change their lives.

Let me share a story told by Mrs. Betsy Short, the principal of the school Jane worked at, as an example of Jane's love and passion for her kids. Betsy writes in her letter to the staff and teachers at Morgan County Primary School titled "God's Grace." '

Jane came to work early every morning and usually stopped by my office to say hello and to share a new website she'd discovered. "I've got a new website to share with you. This is so cool. Here, let me sit at your computer, and I'll show it to you. It will just take a minute..." Thirty minutes later, we would still be sitting side by side, checking out the website. Our conversation usually ended with Jane asking, "Is it OK if I send this link out to everyone? I wanted you to see it first and to give the OK before I sent it out." Jane, ever respectful, always asked me to check websites first.

"Of course, Jane, everyone needs this website", was my usual reply.

Sometimes, it wasn't a website Jane wanted to share. Occasionally, it was a book. "Have you read this book?" Jane would ask. If I had read it, we would discuss the ideas. If I had not read the book, she would thrust it into my hand, and say, "You've got to read it. You are going to be wowed." I'm happy to say I shared a few books and articles with Jane that she hadn't read, but it was rare to find one Jane had not devoured.

Often, Jane came to say, "I've got this idea about helping a student. What do you think?" We always figured out a way to implement her innovative ideas, personalized for the child's needs.

Jane had secrets, too. I promised to keep those secrets, but now, I'm going to give up the goods on Jane and let her secrets out. There comes a time when it is OK to break a confidence, and now we have arrived at that time for some of Jane's secrets. Jane popped in my office one morning, sat down, and said, "I've been thinking...what if we put all of the collaboratives in one cluster? You know, it's our kids that struggle the hardest and take the longest to master skills. If we were all in one cluster, we wouldn't hold any of the other classes back, and we would have more people to help each other. What do you think?"

I thought it was a good idea, but I wanted more time to consider all of the possibilities and to discuss it with Dr. Nash and Brillo. Then Jane added, "Please don't tell anyone it is my idea. Just say it's something for us to think about. I don't want anyone to know I came up with that. They already think I'm a know-it-all." As you know, we had many discussions about this idea. Initially, our decision was to pilot the plan in First Grade the following year to see how well it worked, but when Second Grade heard the plan, they clamored to do the same.

After we decided to group all First and second Grade collaborative classes into one cluster, I mentioned I was concerned about those students not having enough high-achieving student models. Jane came back with another idea, "Let's put the Gifted kids in our collaborative cluster. That will give our kids more high-achieving models, but it will also give Special Ed teachers another perspective too. We can get great instructional ideas from the Gifted teacher."

I liked Jane's idea, but again, she said, "Don't tell anyone that was my idea, please. They don't need to know." I argued that she deserved the credit. "No, I don't", Jane insisted, "Besides, if it doesn't work, you get the blame if they don't know where it came from!" Of course, Jane thought that was funny and giggled all the way up to the Hill Building, I'm sure.

Jane visited many more times with suggestions. "I think it's a good idea to place all of the retained students in our cluster", she suggested. "Some may need more time and a slower pace. We can offer that. Others can move a bit quicker, and they will know a lot about First Grade to help some of our Special Needs kids. They will feel important and will have a chance to be the leaders. It's a win-win for everyone". When we decided to implement this idea, Jane cautioned, "Please don't tell anyone this is my idea." Exasperated, I asked, "Well, just who does get the credit for all of these great ideas, Jane?" She smiled and said, "Who has to get any credit? Just say it's a thought. "

Once again, I was sworn to secrecy. I thought I had her when I told her I would put her on the bottom of the Smart Board list if she told anyone she was on the list. But now Jane had me. "If you tell anyone, I won't share anymore of my ideas!"

Jane loved her work, she loved her kids, and she truly lived a YES life in the NO world of a child with special needs. Life was great for Jane and me, and then in October of 2006 our YES world was shattered when we were told that Jane has advanced breast cancer and they needed to remove her left breast. A person's YES world can quickly turn into a NO world when that six-letter word, CANCER, enters into the picture. As we sat in the recovery room, we expected the doctor to come in and tell us that she had removed all of the cancer, but we never heard those words. The doctor told us that she had removed the breast, she had removed all of the nodes, and she was not positive that she had gotten all of the cancer— she would know more once the results came back...The results indicated that the last node contained cancer, and Jane would have to undergo extensive chemotherapy and radiation treatments.

After many tears Jane looked into my eyes and said, "I am sorry, Mickey." That is Jane, always thinking of the other person in every situation. She had a heart of love for God and for others.

I replied, "I love you Jane, we will do whatever it takes." She claimed that she was looking forward to chemo and radiation because she was ready to "get the show on the road." Over the next few weeks before Jane began her treatments, we discussed our lives with cancer and how we were going to live. Jane loved her kids, and they brought joy and happiness into her life. We examined our work weeks to see how we could make this new adventure work. Our faith was in Jesus Christ, and we believed that if this was our lot, Jesus Christ would be with us and get us through it all. We made a decision that if Christ would open the doors, we would alter our schedules in such a way that Jane would not have to miss any school days. We felt that the love she received from her kids and the positive influence of her friends and co-workers at school were just as important as her chemotherapy and radiation treatments.

Our new schedule would be for Jane to receive her chemo treatments late on Wednesday afternoons. The nature of her treatments allowed her to continue to work at the school on Thursday and Friday, and then the side-effects of the chemotherapy took hold of her body and she would suffer all day on Saturday. Many times she would never get out of bed because of the lack of energy, pain in her legs and arms, and inability to retain food and liquids. On Sundays she would support me in my new calling as senior pastor at a small church. We would eat lunch, and then she would return to bed Sunday afternoon to get the rest she would need to teach her kids the next week.

During all of this, Jane would find the inner strength to research solutions for her kids and the struggles they lived with. She did not want anyone to know her routine, because she felt she would receive special treatment, and she did not want that. If someone asked Jane how she was feeling, she answered, "Just fine. I'm great! Every day is a little better!" So for the next two years we lived this YES routine in our NO world so that Jane could live life to the fullest. For Jane, life to the fullest *was teaching her kids new skills and helping them become all that God has created them to be. And she supported American Cancer Society's Relay for Life, serving as a committee member to show her support of those still fighting cancer.*

Jane endured two years of chemotherapy before she received the great news in the fall of 2008 that her cancer was in remission. Jane's body was never free of cancer. The cancer would go into remission, and as our doctor explained, that meant that it was not advancing in her body. For one year, the cancer was in remission. But as the 2009-2010 school year began, we were told that the cancer was back. It had advanced into Jane's hip and esophagus. Meanwhile, Jane continued to share technology tricks, instructional ideas, and plans for individual students. She participated in cluster meetings and team meetings and taught others the tricks of teaching Special Needs children. All the while, she fought the cancer that was invading her body without her permission.

During the fall of 2010, things in Jane's body changed. She was having problems breathing, and our doctor discovered that the cancer had moved into her lungs. Jane would share with her friends, "I'm positive I will beat this. The chemo helps." The principal at school asked what she could do to make work easier. "Nothing," Jane responded. "I'm no different from anyone else. I don't need anything special." Dr. Short later shared with me that she worried about that, but I also knew teachers in Jane's cluster would respond to her needs when the time came...

And they did. One noticed Jane was struggling walking to The Hill every morning. The Hill was the name fondly given to the building where Jane's classroom was. Jane's fellow teachers asked that Jane to be allowed to park behind the cottages so she wouldn't have to walk so far. Many of Jane's fellow teachers stepped up to take over Jane's duties so she didn't have to stand or come down to the main building. It was evident to her friends at her school that she continued to struggle with the invasion of cancer in her lungs. By November of 2010, Jane was being assisted by a portable oxygen tank so that she could continue to teach her kids each day. The teachers rallied around Jane and moved their Team Meetings in Jane's classroom so she didn't have to walk anywhere. Dr. Short later shared with me that the fact that Jane did not argue with these requests scared her. It scared me as well. I knew that Jane was struggling at home, but I always figured our plan that would allow her to continue at school without special treatment was still moving forward as planned.

Dr. Short shared with me this moment she had with Jane one morning just before the Thanksgiving break:

Jane walked to my office early one morning, and I chastised her for not calling for me to come to her classroom. "There's no way I'm beeping the office to tell the principal to come to me," she joked. We had a long discussion about her illness, and she mentioned the possibility that I did not wish to discuss, but Jane was determined to have this conversation. You know what that meant. She was not letting me off the hook, and she had a lot of questions. Once again, she forced me into secrecy. I promised I would never share with others how sick she really was, no matter how sick she became. She assured me if she were sick at home or in the hospital, she would send positive emails to everyone. She intended to fight for life all the way. "If I have five more minutes to live, I want it to be the best five minutes ever," Jane said. At the end of our conversation, she added, "When I'm gone, I want you to write about me and you can tell them anything you want to then."

Jane continued to live a YES life in the NO world of cancer. She wanted to live. In April of 2010, she was blessed with her first grandchild. Once our girls had grown up, we talked about our desire to spoil our grandchildren. And Jane now had her first grandchild, and she wanted to live to see him grow up. Jane did not like to have her picture taken, but every time she was holding her grandson, she wanted her picture taken. She would look at the pictures of her and her grandson during those anxious times when she was not able to catch her breath. She never complained about the pain when she was playing with her grandson. She always smiled and laughed, and with every ounce of strength she had, she would create memory moments for her grandson to remember her.

Christmas 2010 was filled with hours of laughter and joy as Jane played with her grandson and enjoyed her family and friends. Yet Christmas 2010 was also filled with hours of pain and anxiety as Jane continued her fight against this evil disease that was taking her life away from her and others.

My job as her caregiver was to protect her life—protect her integrity so that others did not know the intensity of the fight she was in. She did not want others to feel sorry for her. She never wanted others to know the dark side of her life, because if they did, she felt that it would cause her to begin to live a NO life in this NO world. And she was determined not to allow this evil disease to take her positive YES attitude away from her.

After a wonderful Christmas with her family and friends, January 2011 began a new phase of her fight to remain YES in her NO world. It became more difficult for Jane to breathe. The NO world began to cause her to have horrifying anxiety attacks. Fluid built up in and around her lungs. We would have her lungs drained and within three days, the fluid would return. I wish I could say I was the ideal caretaker. I was not. Many times, the frustration of watching the love of my life struggle to breathe brought out anger and negative reactions. I felt unable to help this wonderful, positive, inspirational woman who had blessed *me with two beautiful girls and a life filled with memories that continue to bless me to this day.*

Yet through it all, Jane would ask, "We are going to defeat this, right?"

And I would respond, "Yes, Baby, yes. We are going to defeat this evil."

She would smile and say to me, "Make sure you take care of my kids. I want my kids to get through this knowing that they are loved."

Jane returned to school after the Christmas break and continued to life a YES life in her NO world. After a brief light of hope when it seemed as if the chemotherapy was causing the cancer to retreat, Jane was diagnosed with pneumonia and hospitalized for five days. While in the hospital, she requested that I bring her laptop to the hospital so that she could send emails to her friends at school. In one email she relayed this message, "My sister has heard my cries, and has organized my escape. Jessi will cause a distraction with all of the frogs everyone has sent me, Mickey will have the getaway car, and when they are not looking, I will make a break and be back in the classroom on Monday." Well she escaped. She returned to the classroom, and received much needed love from her kids.

On the following Sunday, as I prepared to go to church, Jane was suffering through one of her worst anxiety attacks and was unable to breathe. I rushed her to the emergency room. They placed her on a breathing machine that she hated. Her blood-oxygen level was critical, and against her desires, I chose to have her placed on life-support. This allowed her children and family, those who were able to, to come and say their last goodbyes. Yet, even while Jane was on life-support, when the nurse reduced the drug that kept her asleep, she would communicate in a positive way and would always think of others. Even on her death bed, Jane lived a YES life in a NO world.

It was her choice to say YES when the world wanted her to say NO. For example, when she told me that Monday was

Valentine's Day, and she wanted her kids to receive a Valentine's gift from her. Each time she was able, she would ask if I had made sure that her kids would get a Valentine's from her. After I assured her, she would then relax and enjoy time with family and friends. When the anxiety returned, visitors would leave and allow Jane and me to experience the love that we had shared throughout the five years that we lived YES in response to the NO we had been dealt by this evil world.

On the Saturdays that Jane suffered with the side-effects of chemotherapy, during the days and nights that Jane struggled to breathe and anxiety caused fear to grab hold of her, and through these last moments of her life as the evil of cancer literally took her breath away, I would assist her as she took a journey, led by the Holy Spirit, to a safe place, a place we called Jane's Happy Place, to allow Jane to enter into the presence of Jesus Christ, the only one with the power of love that could remove all fear and anxiety and bring her to a state of peace.

Please allow me to describe this place, as God allowed me to see it, the morning before Jesus dressed Jane in her new, resurrected, immortal body.

There is a field of flowing flowers in a cool breeze. To the east there is the beach at St. Simons—Epworth by the Sea. To the west is the snow covered peak of Mt. Evans—Denver, Colo. Flowing from the north to the south is the river of life, flowing out of the New Jerusalem, a small stream of cold purified water cascading over moss-covered stones smoothed by 52 years of the love of Jesus Christ. Falling over the stream is a branch of a Live Oak tree with a soft blanket draped to sit upon. Next to the stream is a small path that leads up to the branch and away from the branch. There are birds singing the praise of life and love. There are small animals frolicking and playing in the flowers, laughing and giggling as they enjoy the warmth coming from the glowing face of Jesus Christ who is sitting on the branch.

Sitting next to Jesus was a green frog. Jesus looks at me, smiles, points to the frog, and says to me, "Frog E." The joy of *understanding fills my heart, for during Jane's five-year struggle with cancer she was never alone; Jesus was with her the whole time. For Frog E was sent by Jesus to love, comfort, strengthen and fill Jane with peace and joy until this day would come. Then I see Jane walking down the path towards the branch where Jesus is sitting. Jesus stretches out his muscular arms, and invites Jane to sit next to him. As Jane sits down, Jesus smiles and wraps his arms around Jane. A smile of contentment and fulfillment comes upon both faces. Jane rests her weary head on his shoulder, closes her eyes, and peace covers her face. Jane raises her head and a radiant beauty, unlike I have ever seen, shines from her face as she looks into the eyes of Jesus Christ. With their feet dangling in the cool waters of the running stream, and the sounds of the water over the rocks, I see them talking. What they are saying I cannot tell, but their conversation is filled with moments of laughter, smiles, hugs and tears of pure joy.*

Then I hear Jesus say to Jane, "The time has come." Jane looks directly at me, and my spirit reads her lips. She smiles and says "Thank you." Then Jesus takes Jane's hand into his big strong hand and they stand up on the branch and begin to walk down the path.

I shout to Jane, "Way to go, Baby, way to go. I love you!" Jane and Jesus begin skipping down the path laughing, singing, and dancing. Hopping beside them is Frog E. As they fade into the distance, the shape of two joy-filled figures slowly turns into a bright glow. A peace consumes my heart, a joy rushes over me, and I know my Baby, the love of my life, the mother of my two beautiful girls, is completely healed. For Jane has received her resurrection body.

Dr. Short ended her letter of sharing Jane's secrets to the teachers and staff of Morgan County Primary School with these words:

By the way, *Jane* is a Hebrew name that means *God's grace.* We witnessed God's grace through Jane daily, before and after her illness. On Friday, February 11, Jane asked her husband to order Valentine cookies for her students to be delivered Monday, February 14. Jane said the cookies would be a gift from Heaven because she knew that is where she would be when the cookies were delivered. You see, Jane decided, along with her family, to remove life support Saturday, February 12. Jane, of course, initiated that decision, thereby relieving her loved ones from that difficult determination. Life support was removed at 10:30 a.m. Saturday, February 12, and Jane passed away, surrounded by her loved ones, without pain or suffering, at 10:38 a.m. Jane was prepared to meet her Father and peacefully did so. Jane, filled with God's grace, was—and still is—a gift from Heaven.

Jane, I love you. The memories you have left me are filled with life, joy, hope and the knowledge of knowing it is worth living a YES life no matter what NO this evil world throws at you.
~T. Mickey Moss

Reflections

I don't think life is a puzzle. I don't think it is a hidden code to be discovered. I see it more as a stained glass window. We are all broken pieces of glass welded together to form a beautiful image—when the light shines through it. Few of us ever end up living the life we thought we would live. But rather than complain, whine or become immobilized we learn to grow. We learn truths we would have never learned without the setback.

I think we are all broken pieces. We hurt. We rebuild. We are richer where we have loved and lost.

I believe we all need grace. It isn't cheap. It isn't a platitude or instant answer. It is a gift to be received.

The beauty of who we are only becomes radiant when we share our brokenness with one another.

In the community of "brokenness" we find love, acceptance and affirmation. When the light of God's grace shines through the places where we don't fit together, where we have been knocked off the road, and where we are inconsistent, we are at home with the One who loves us unconditionally. We have found our place in this world. We have found our home.

Come Walk With Us...

I think we all want to make sense of our lives and find the sacred in the midst of all the chaos. That isn't easy to do even on our best days. What I have discovered is that you don't have to walk alone.

Maybe, you would like to continue this journey, but you don't want to do it by yourself. To those of you who want to walk further, learn more, and become the intentional person you believe you were created to be, there are additional resources for you to consider.

Please visit our website at: www.iliveyes.com. There you will find descriptions of our one-on-one coaching packages that will offer the support and direction you need. You can also read about our retreats and weekly telephone conferences. All of these are intended to offer you encouragement and hope.

One of the goals of this book is that you would not be left alone.

Come join us now! Live YES!

Website: www.iliveyes.com

Email: randy@iliveyes.com

Endnotes

These are some of the resources I have used in developing thoughts and sharing ideas. I am drawn to writers who offer a more reflective approach to faith and life.

[i] Frost, R. (1920). The Road Not Taken. In Mountain Interval. New York. Henry Holt.

[ii] Seasons. In Wikidpedia. Retrieved October 11, 2011. From, http://en.wikipedia.org/wiki/Season.

[iii] Manning, B. (2005). *The Ragamuffin Gospel*. Colorado Springs. Multnomah. P.14.

[iv] Buechner, F. (1991). *Telling Secrets*. New York. HarperCollins Publishers. p.2-3.

[v] Gibran. K. (1973). Your Children Are Not Your Own. In *The Prophet*. Wordsworth Editions. P. 8.

[vi] Forrest Gump. (1994). Directed by Robert Zemeckis. An American comedy-drama film based on the 1986 novel of the same name by Winston Groom.

[vii] Frank and Ernest. Comic character created by Bob Thaves

[viii] Garrison Keillor. The Prairie Home Companion. The News from Lake Wobegon.

[ix] Energizer Bunny. Marketing icon for Energizer Batteries.

[x] Rilke, R. (1993). *Letters to a Young Poet*. W.W. Norton & Company. Revised edition.

[xi] Ball, P. Ryan. Live the Questions. Blog The Healing Walk. Retrieved from https://thehealingwalk.wordpress.com/20ten/09/01/live-the-questions/The Healing Walk. March 9, 2011.

[xii] *The Wizard of Oz.* A 1939 American film directed by Victor Fleming. It was based upon the 1900 children's novel, *The Wonderful Wizard of Oz* by L. Frank Baum.

[xiii] Manning. B. (2002). *Ruthless Trust.* New York. HarperCollins. p. 3-4.

[xiv] (Guy Sayles, personal communication. n.d.)

[xv] CNN Staff Wire Staff. (July 10, 2011). Kidnap Victim Jaycee Dugard Talks about Her 18 years of Terror; Retrieved from http://articles.cnn.com/2011-07-10/us/dugard.abc.interview_1_jaycee-dugard-phillip-garrido-nancy-garrido?_s=PM:US. On August, 2011.

[xvi] Hugo. V. Les Miserable. A play based upon the book.

[xvii] U. S. Route 129. In http://en.wikipedia.org/wiki/U.S._Route_129. Accessed September 8, 2011.

[xviii] Elliott. T.S. Little Giddings. In Four Quartets. Quoted by Guy Sayles in personal communication. n.d. 2011.

[xix] Sayles, G. (Private Communication, n.d.)

[xx] Palmer. P. 1990. *The Active Life: A Spirituality of Work, Creativity and Caring.* San Francisco: Jossey-Bass.

[xxi] Extreme Home Makeover. ABC. Aired October, 2011.

[xxii] The Kennedy Center Honors. December 5, 2010. http://www.kennedy-center.org/events/?event=XLHON

[xxiii] Manning. B. 1996. *The Signature of Jesus. Colorado Springs.* Multnomah. P. 14.

xxiv Manning, B. 2009. The *Furious Longing of God*. Colorado Springs. David C. Cook. P. 12.

xxvManning. B. The Ragamuffin Gospel.

xxvi Sayles, G. *The Promise of Home*. Facebook communication. Accessed on May 18, 2011 at 6:44am.

xxvii Sayles, G. *The Promise of Home*.

CPSIA information can be obtained at www.ICGtesting.com
Printed in the USA
LVOW12s1227121114

413310LV00002B/40/P